GRAPHIC HISTORY: WARRIORS

MEDIEVAL KNIGHTS

EUROPE'S FEARSOME ARMORED SOLDIERS

By Blake Hoena
Illustrated by János Orbán

Consultant:
Tim Solie
Adjunct Professor of History
Minnesota State University, Mankato
Mankato, Minnesota

CAPSTONE PRESS
a capstone imprint

Graphic Library is published by Capstone Press,
1710 Roe Crest Drive, North Mankato, Minnesota 56003
www.mycapstone.com

Library of Congress Cataloging-in-Publication data
Names: Hoena, B. A., author. | Orbán, János, illustrator.
Title: Medieval knights : Europe's fearsome armored soldiers / by Blake Hoena;
   illustrated by János Orbán.
Description: North Mankato, Minnesota : Capstone Press, 2019. | Series: Graphic history:
   Warriors | "Graphic Library." | Includes bibliographical references and index.
Identifiers: LCCN 2018031746 (print) | LCCN 2018035351 (ebook) | ISBN 9781543555103
   (eBook PDF) | ISBN 9781543555011 (library binding) | ISBN 9781543559286 (paperback)
Subjects: LCSH: Knights and knighthood—Juvenile literature. | Knights and knighthood—
   Comic books, strips, etc. | Civilization, Medieval—Juvenile literature. | Civilization,
   Medieval—Comic books, strips, etc. | Middle Ages—Juvenile literature. | Middle Ages—
   Comic books, strips, etc. | Graphic novels.
Classification: LCC CR4513 (ebook) | LCC CR4513 .H64 2019 (print) | DDC 929.7/1—dc23
LC record available at https://lccn.loc.gov/2018031746

Summary: In graphic novel format, tells several tales of famous knights while exploring the
history, armor, weapons, and battles of these fearsome warriors from medieval Europe.

EDITOR
Aaron J. Sautter

ART DIRECTOR
Nathan Gassman

DESIGNER
Ted Williams

MEDIA RESEARCHER
Jo Miller

PRODUCTION SPECIALIST
Kathy McColley

Design Elements
Shutterstock: michelaubryphoto, Reinhold Leitner

Printed and bound in the United states of America.
PA48

TABLE OF CONTENTS

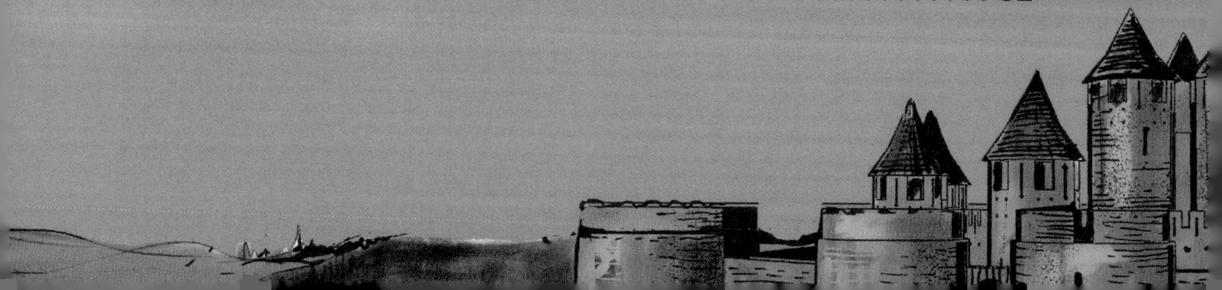

THE RISE OF MEDIEVAL KNIGHTS

At the start of the Middle Ages, infantry units were the dominant military force. Foot soldiers could fight more easily holding both shields and weapons than mounted warriors.

CHARGE!

But when stirrups were introduced to Europe in the 700s, things began to change. These loops hung from each side of a horse's saddle. Riders used them to support their feet as they charged into battle.

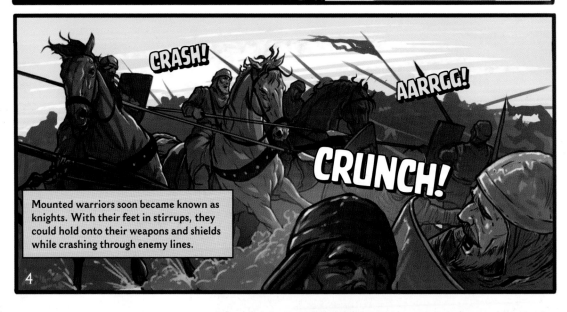

CRASH!

AARRGG!

CRUNCH!

Mounted warriors soon became known as knights. With their feet in stirrups, they could hold onto their weapons and shields while crashing through enemy lines.

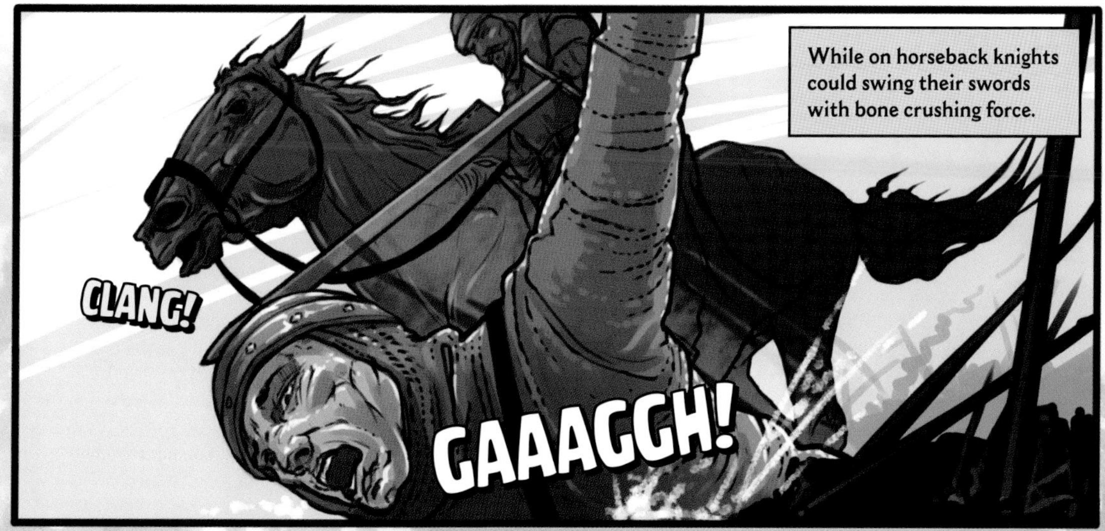
While on horseback knights could swing their swords with bone crushing force.
CLANG!
GAAAGGH!

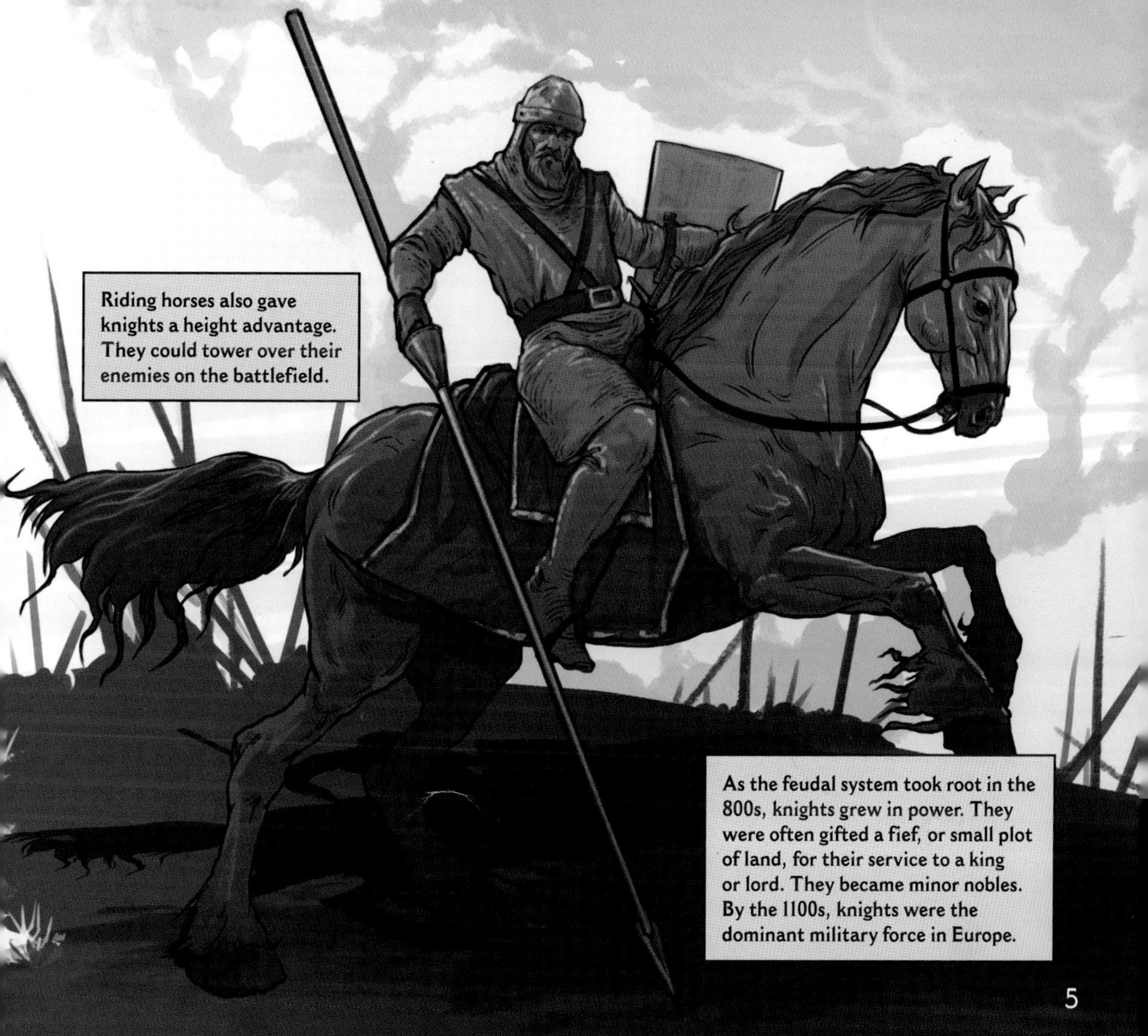
Riding horses also gave knights a height advantage. They could tower over their enemies on the battlefield.
As the feudal system took root in the 800s, knights grew in power. They were often gifted a fief, or small plot of land, for their service to a king or lord. They became minor nobles. By the 1100s, knights were the dominant military force in Europe.

THE KNIGHTING OF JAMES DOUGLAS

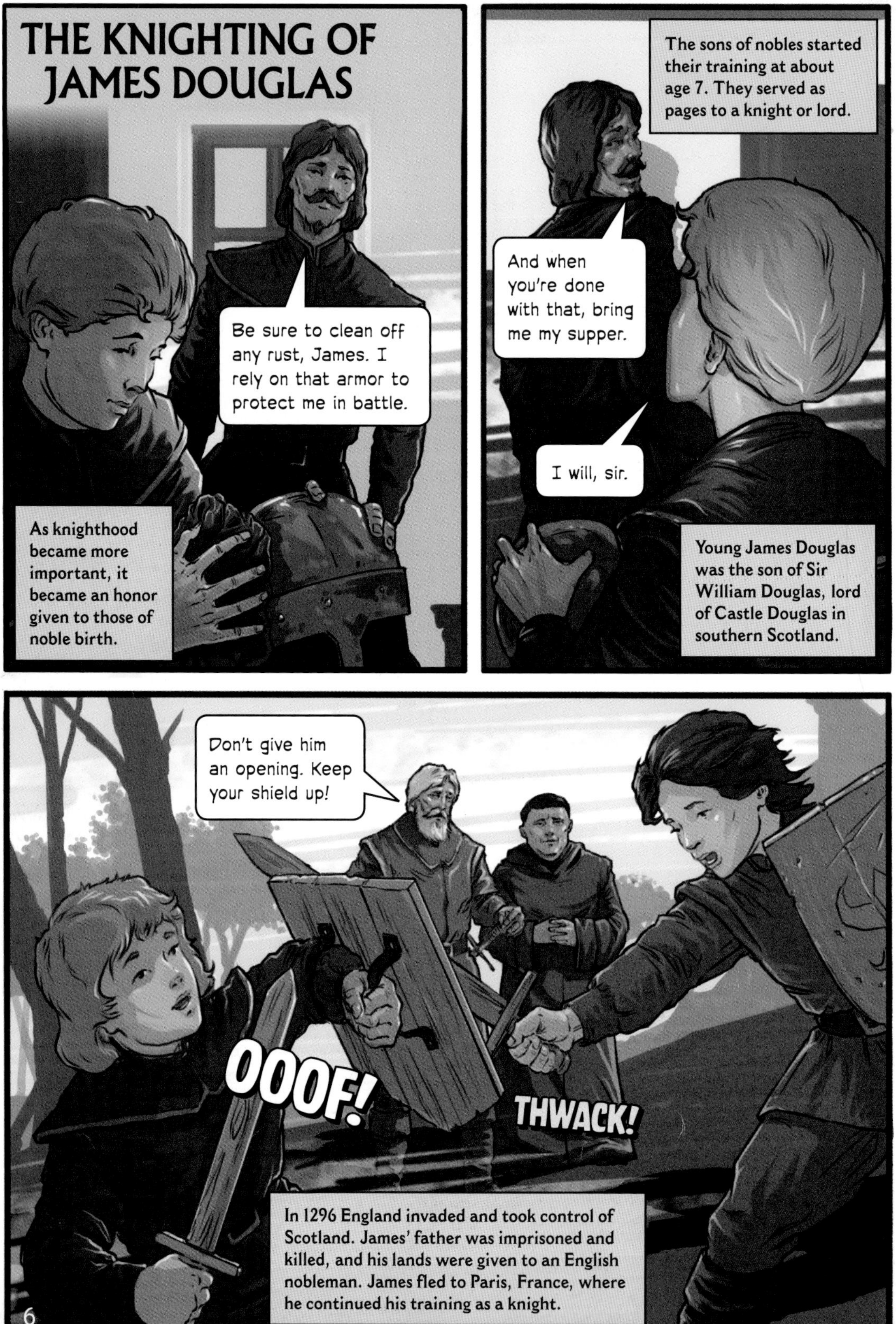
Be sure to clean off any rust, James. I rely on that armor to protect me in battle.
As knighthood became more important, it became an honor given to those of noble birth.
The sons of nobles started their training at about age 7. They served as pages to a knight or lord.
And when you're done with that, bring me my supper.
I will, sir.
Young James Douglas was the son of Sir William Douglas, lord of Castle Douglas in southern Scotland.
Don't give him an opening. Keep your shield up!
OOOF!
THWACK!
In 1296 England invaded and took control of Scotland. James' father was imprisoned and killed, and his lands were given to an English nobleman. James fled to Paris, France, where he continued his training as a knight.

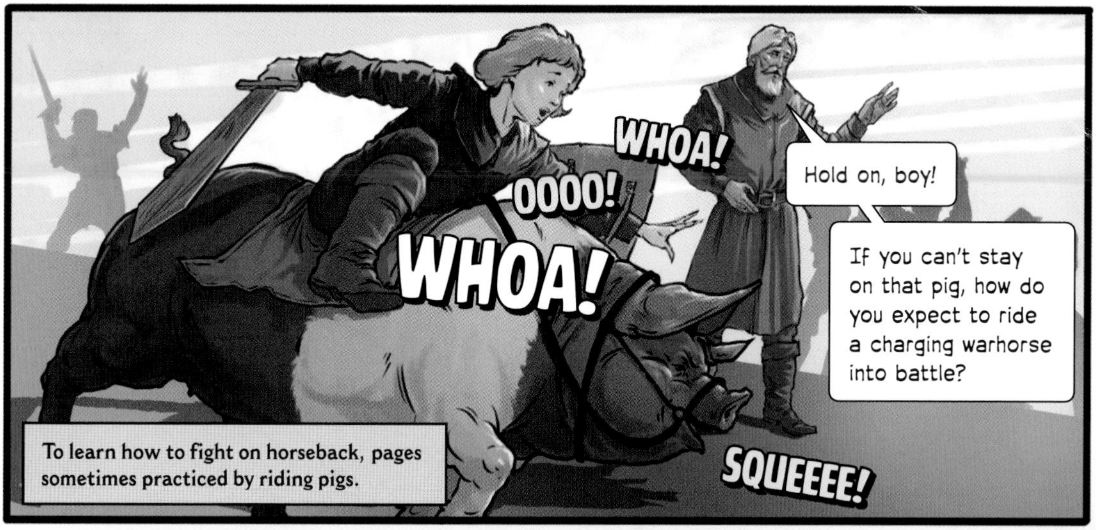

To learn how to fight on horseback, pages sometimes practiced by riding pigs.
WHOA!
OOOO!
WHOA!
Hold on, boy!
If you can't stay on that pig, how do you expect to ride a charging warhorse into battle?
SQUEEEE!

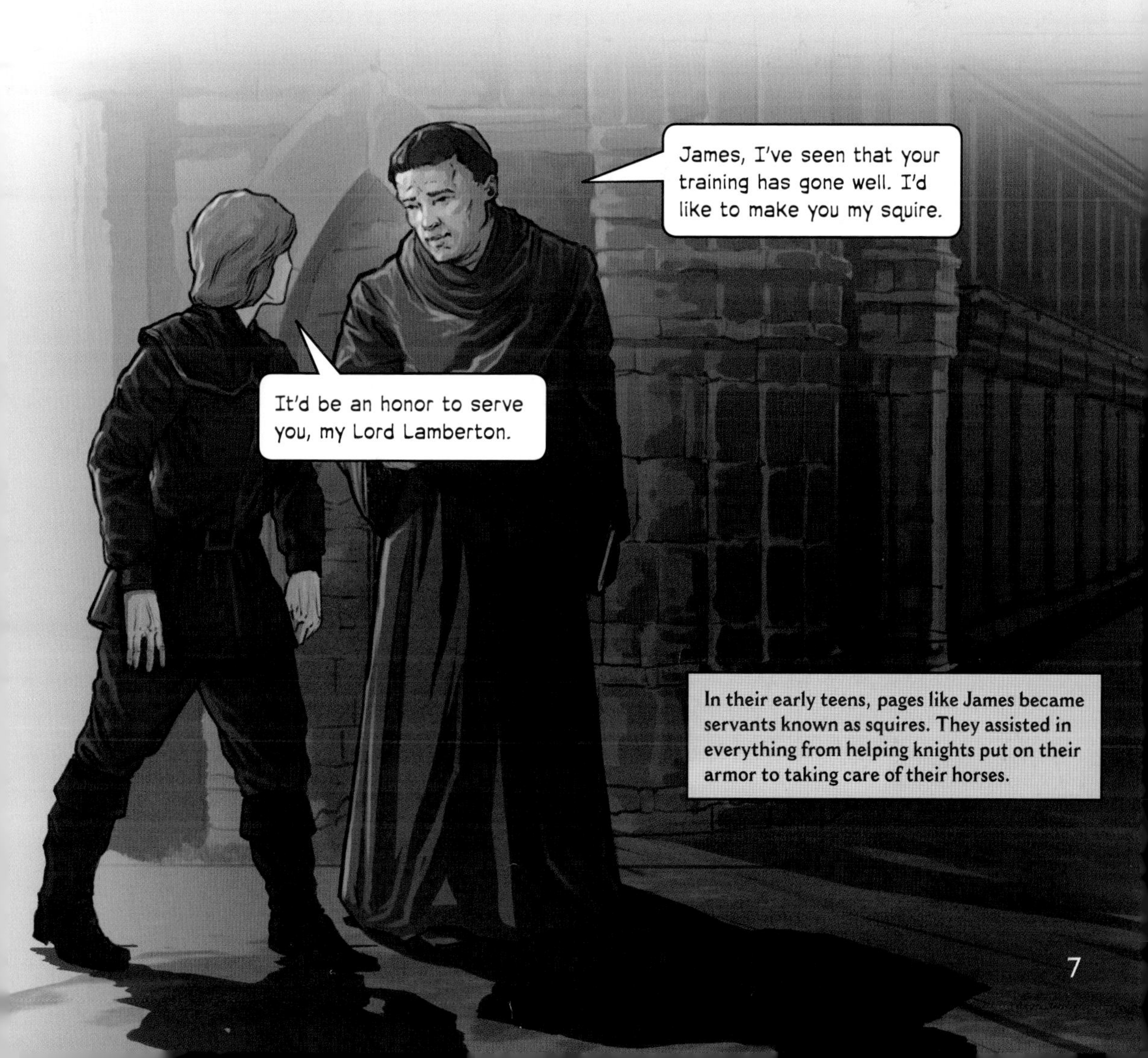

James, I've seen that your training has gone well. I'd like to make you my squire.
It'd be an honor to serve you, my Lord Lamberton.
In their early teens, pages like James became servants known as squires. They assisted in everything from helping knights put on their armor to taking care of their horses.

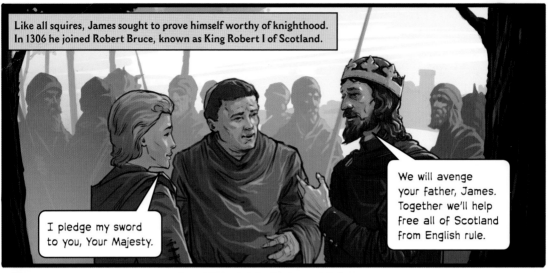

Like all squires, James sought to prove himself worthy of knighthood. In 1306 he joined Robert Bruce, known as King Robert I of Scotland.

We will avenge your father, James. Together we'll help free all of Scotland from English rule.

I pledge my sword to you, Your Majesty.

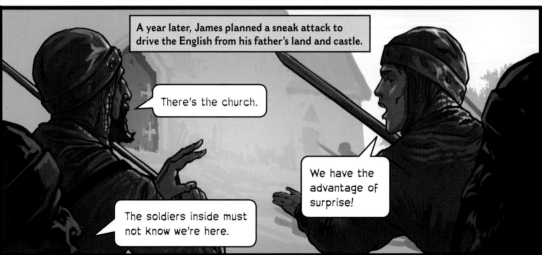

A year later, James planned a sneak attack to drive the English from his father's land and castle.

There's the church.

We have the advantage of surprise!

The soldiers inside must not know we're here.

For Douglas!

For my father!

James attacked on Palm Sunday, when many of the English soldiers were at church services. The fight was quick and bloody.

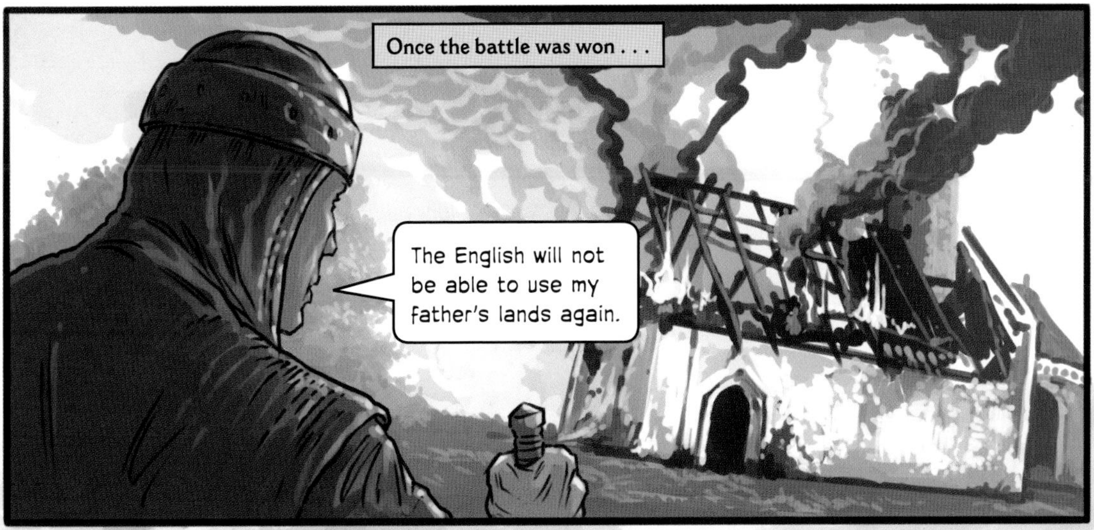
Once the battle was won . . .
The English will not be able to use my father's lands again.

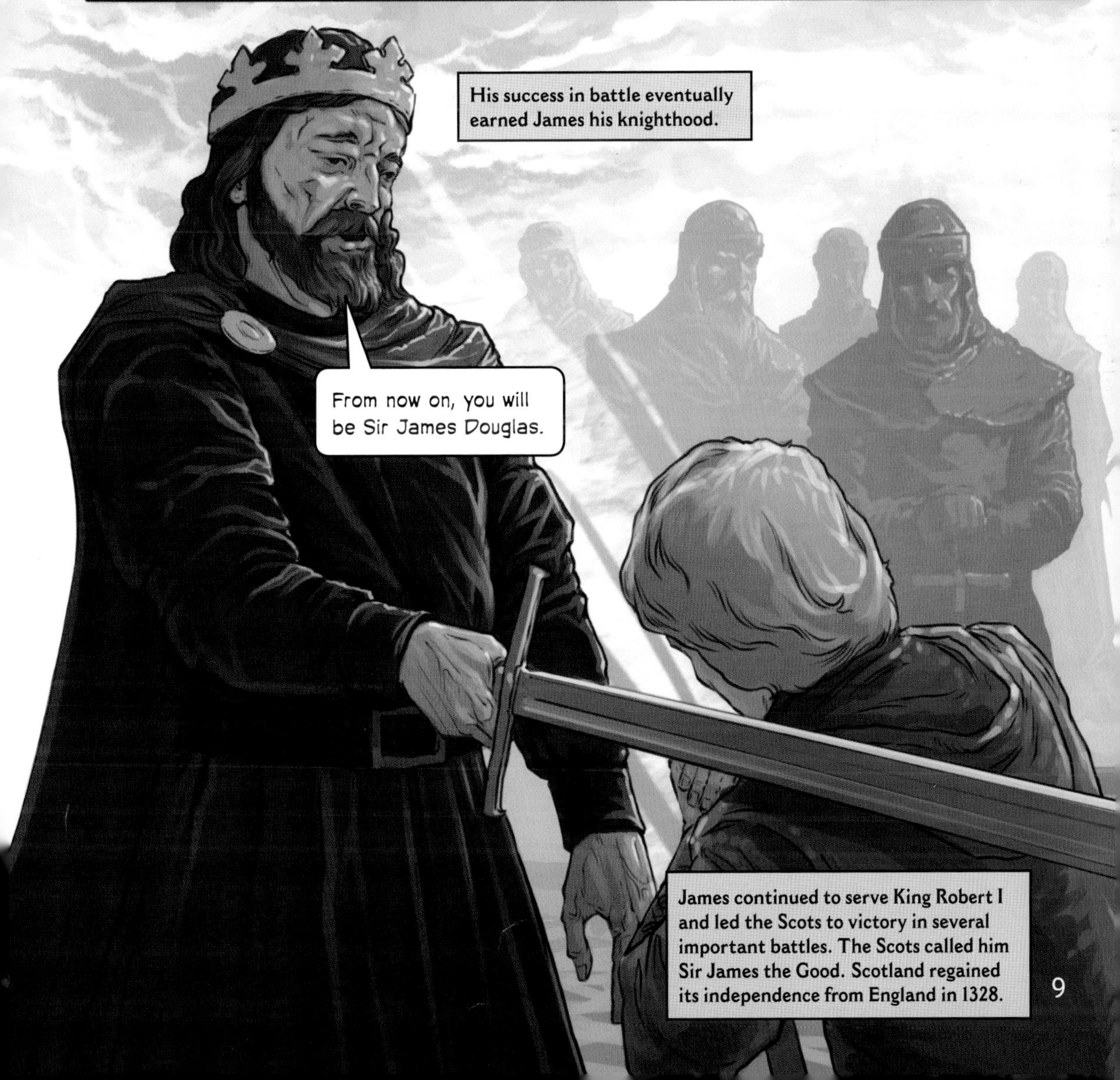
His success in battle eventually earned James his knighthood.
From now on, you will be Sir James Douglas.
James continued to serve King Robert I and led the Scots to victory in several important battles. The Scots called him Sir James the Good. Scotland regained its independence from England in 1328.

WILLIAM MARSHAL, TOURNAMENT CHAMPION

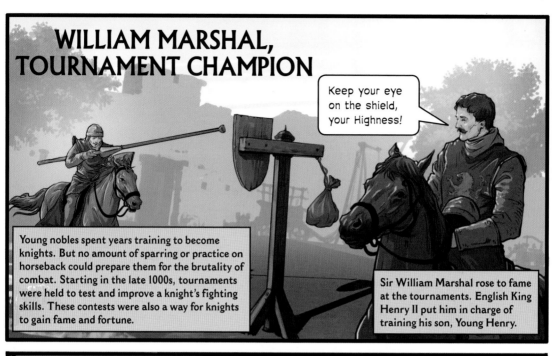

Keep your eye on the shield, your Highness!

Young nobles spent years training to become knights. But no amount of sparring or practice on horseback could prepare them for the brutality of combat. Starting in the late 1000s, tournaments were held to test and improve a knight's fighting skills. These contests were also a way for knights to gain fame and fortune.

Sir William Marshal rose to fame at the tournaments. English King Henry II put him in charge of training his son, Young Henry.

THUNK!

That was a perfect strike!

It was. But you aren't on the tournament field yet. It's not so easy when your opponents are trying to unhorse you.

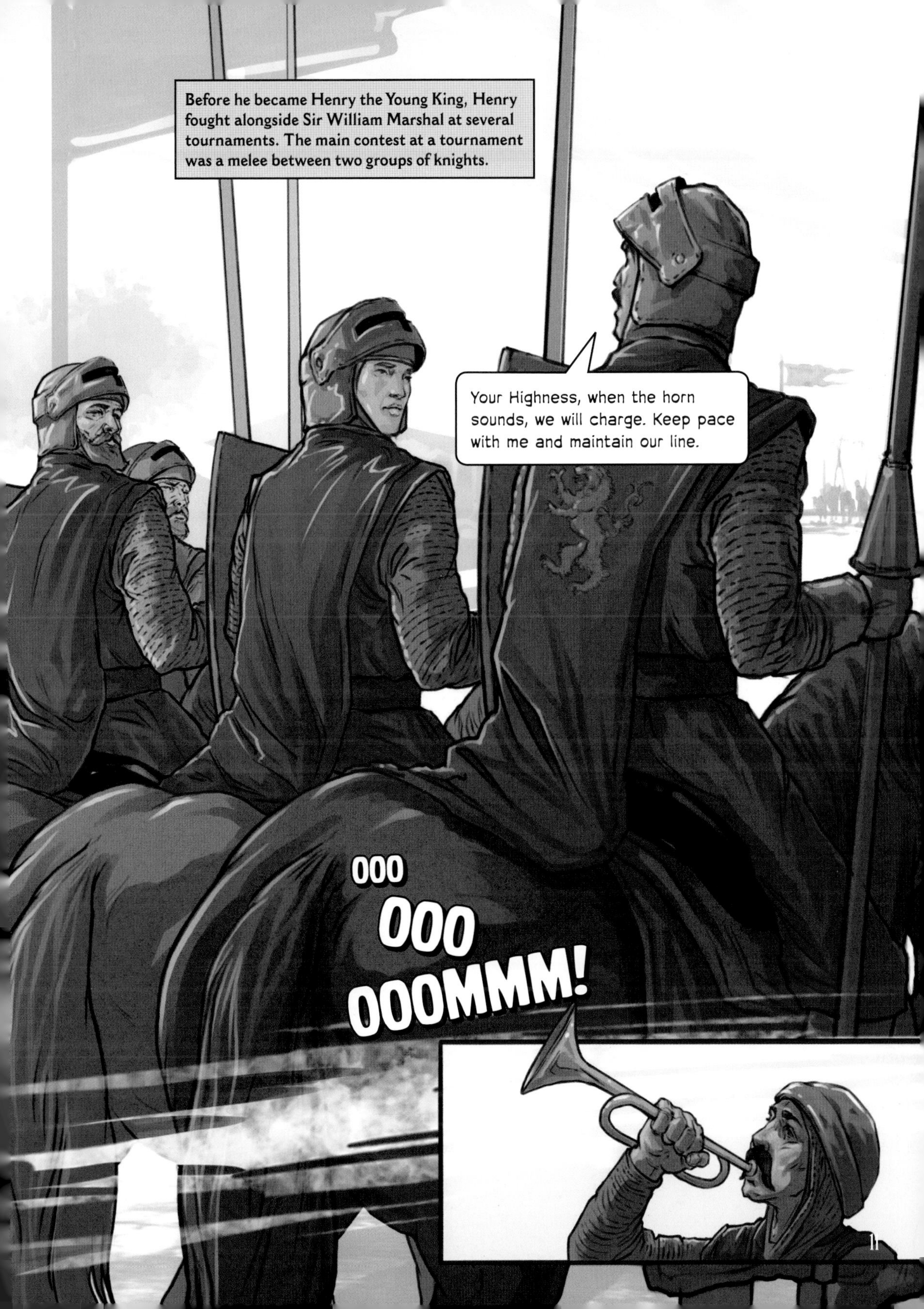

Before he became Henry the Young King, Henry fought alongside Sir William Marshal at several tournaments. The main contest at a tournament was a melee between two groups of knights.
Your Highness, when the horn sounds, we will charge. Keep pace with me and maintain our line.
OOO OOO OOOMMM!

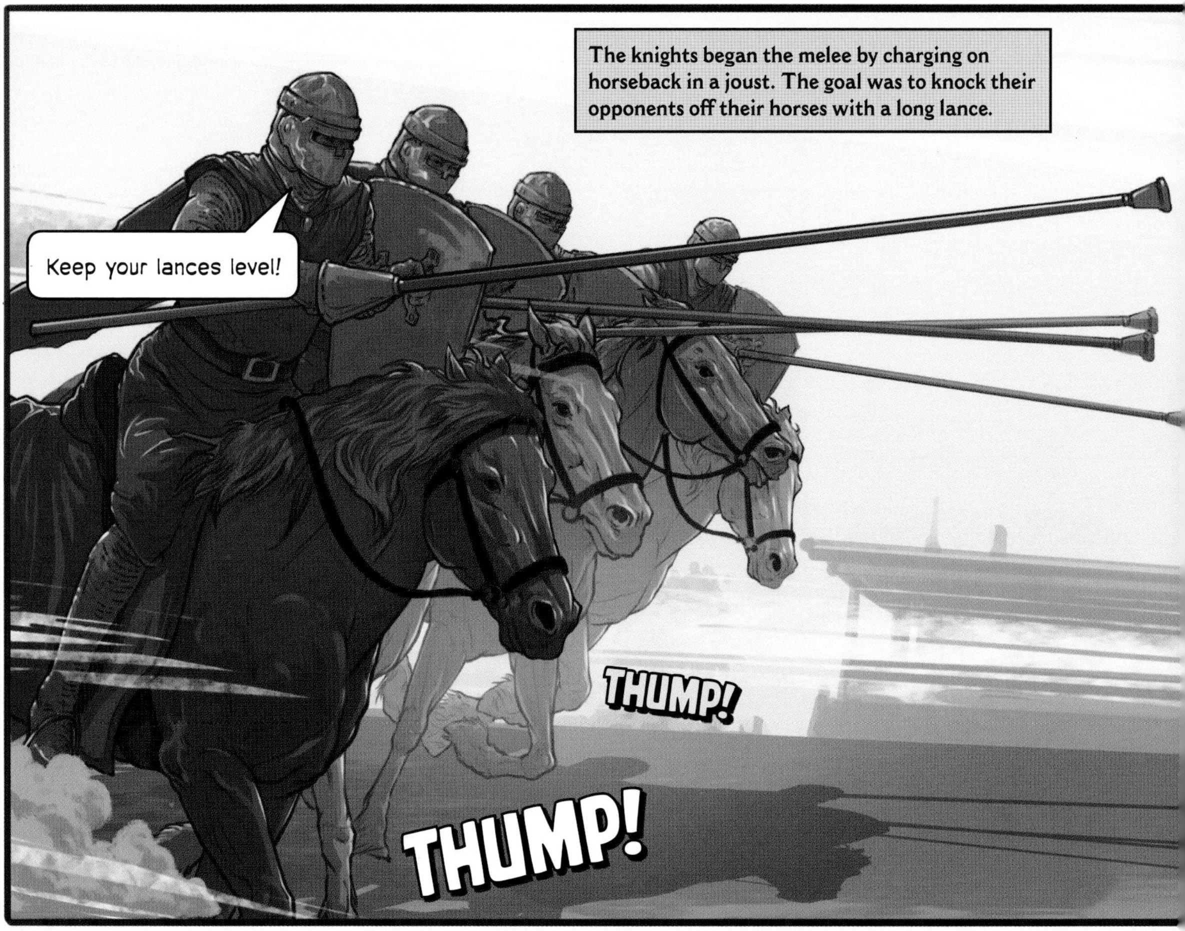
The knights began the melee by charging on horseback in a joust. The goal was to knock their opponents off their horses with a long lance.
Keep your lances level!
THUMP!
THUMP!

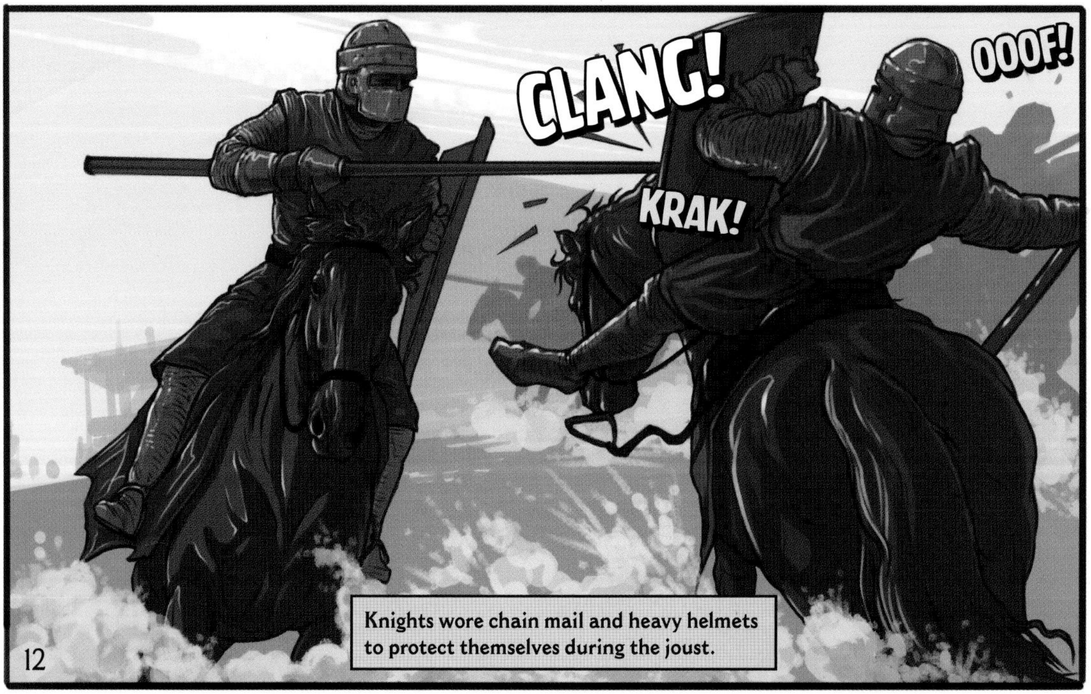
CLANG!
OOOF!
KRAK!
Knights wore chain mail and heavy helmets to protect themselves during the joust.

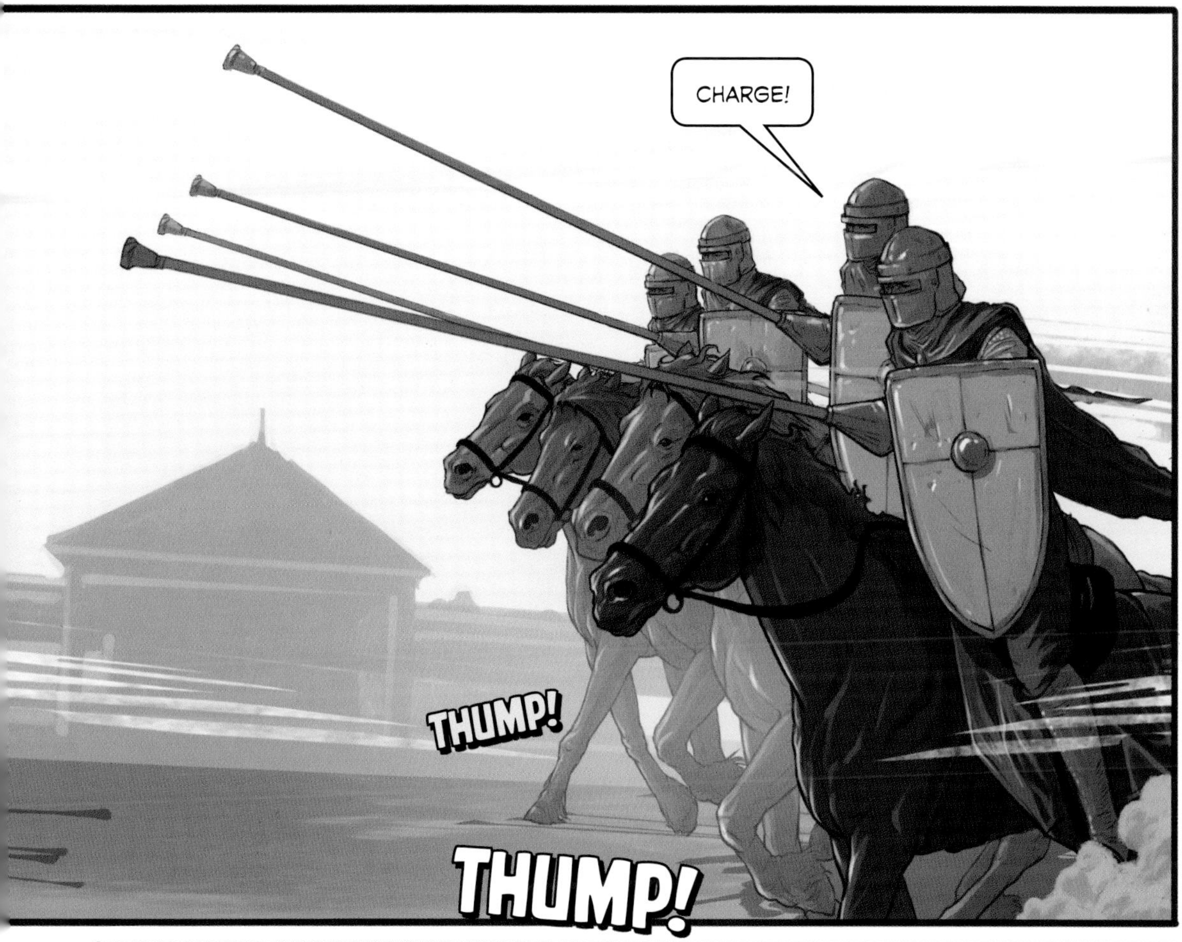
CHARGE!
THUMP!
THUMP!

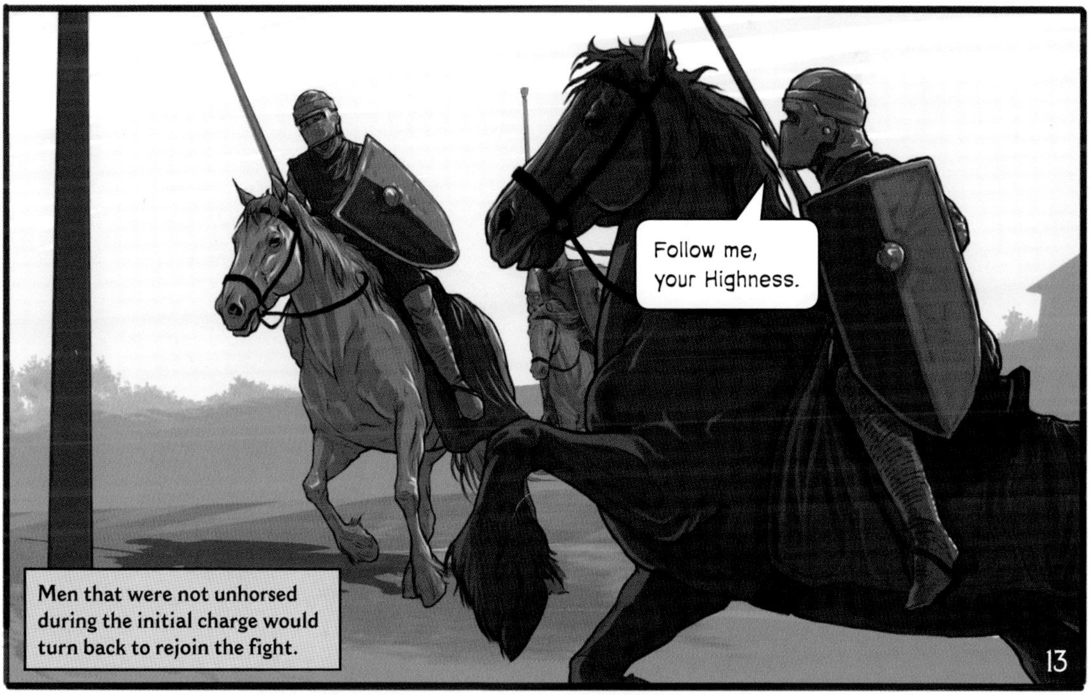
Follow me, your Highness.
Men that were not unhorsed during the initial charge would turn back to rejoin the fight.

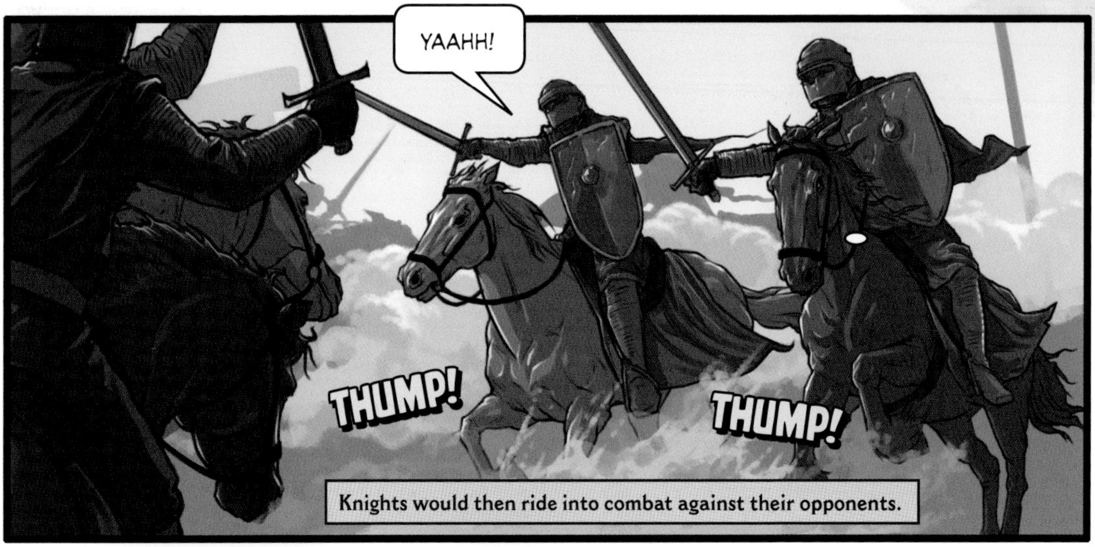
YAAHH!
THUMP!
THUMP!
Knights would then ride into combat against their opponents.

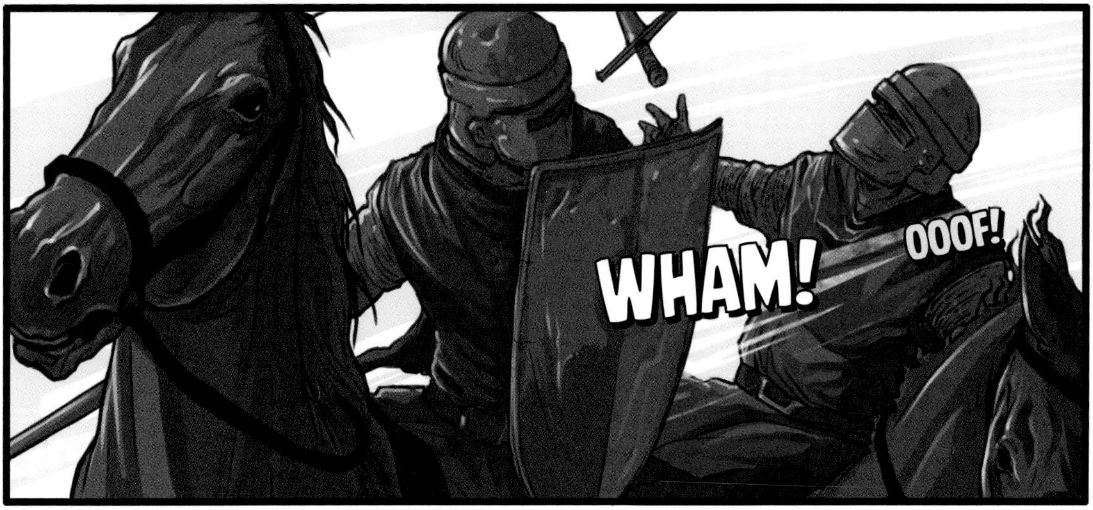
WHAM!
OOOF!

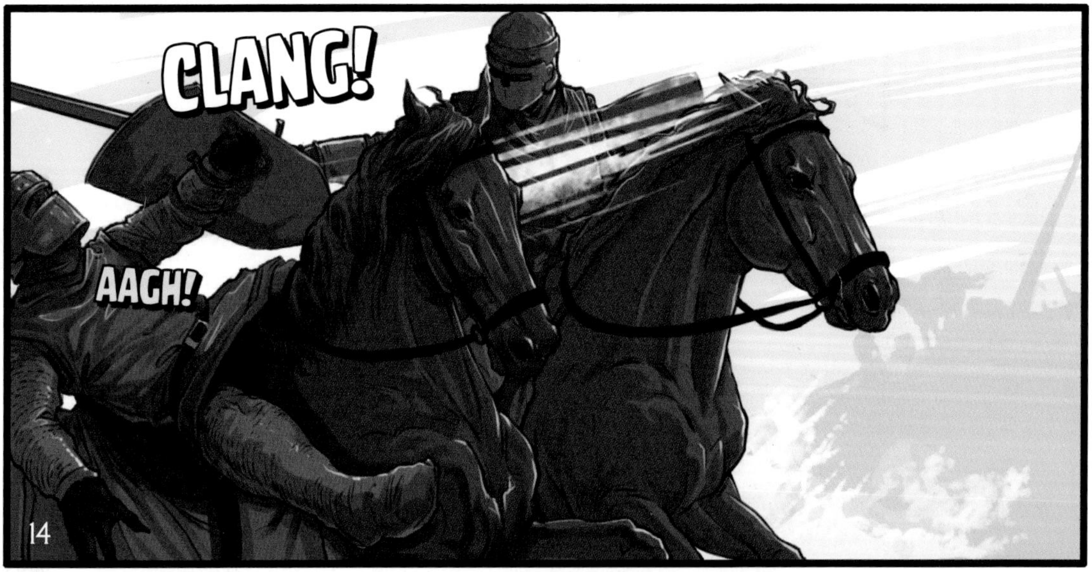
CLANG!
AAGH!

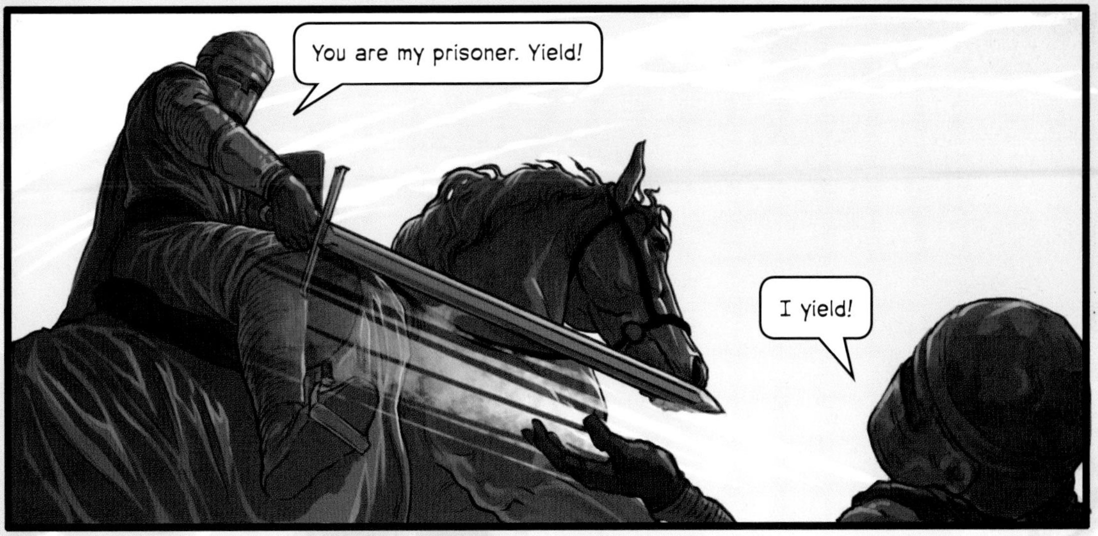
You are my prisoner. Yield!
I yield!

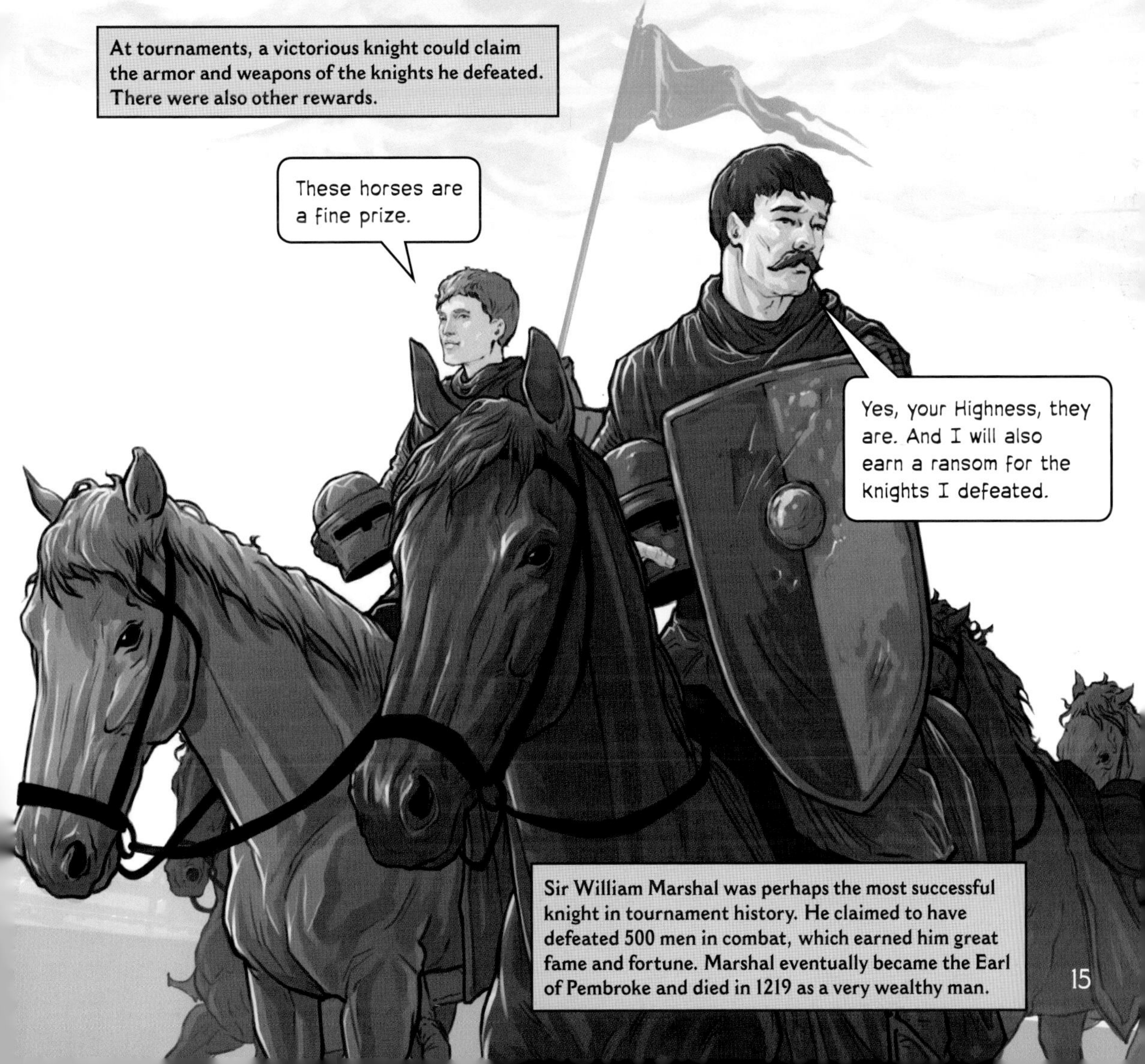
At tournaments, a victorious knight could claim the armor and weapons of the knights he defeated. There were also other rewards.
These horses are a fine prize.
Yes, your Highness, they are. And I will also earn a ransom for the knights I defeated.
Sir William Marshal was perhaps the most successful knight in tournament history. He claimed to have defeated 500 men in combat, which earned him great fame and fortune. Marshal eventually became the Earl of Pembroke and died in 1219 as a very wealthy man.

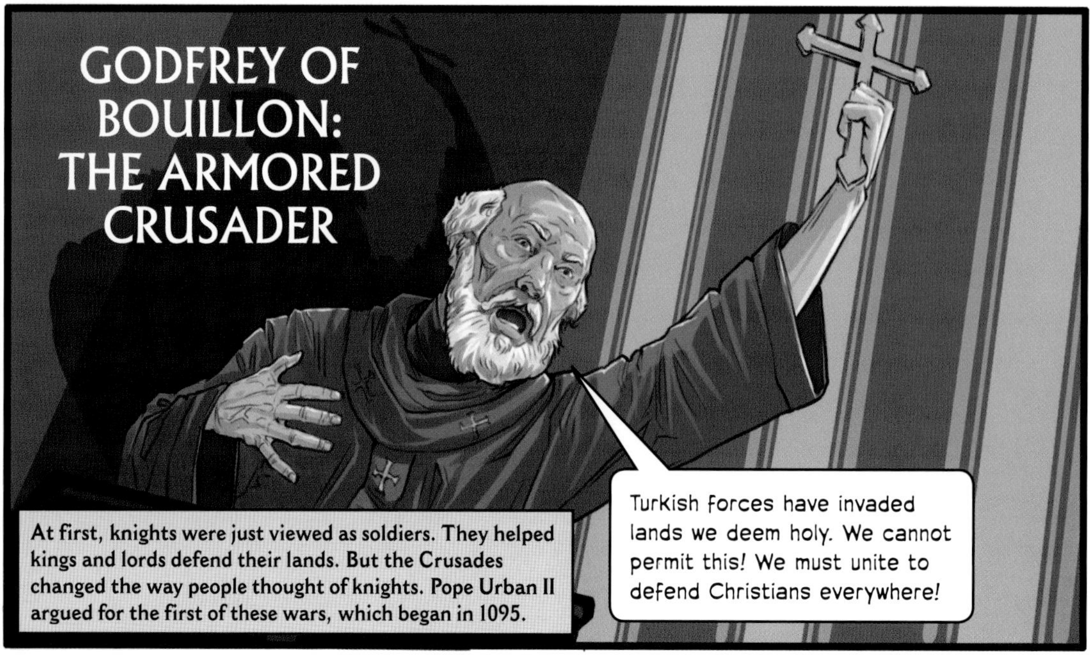
GODFREY OF BOUILLON: THE ARMORED CRUSADER
At first, knights were just viewed as soldiers. They helped kings and lords defend their lands. But the Crusades changed the way people thought of knights. Pope Urban II argued for the first of these wars, which began in 1095.
Turkish forces have invaded lands we deem holy. We cannot permit this! We must unite to defend Christians everywhere!

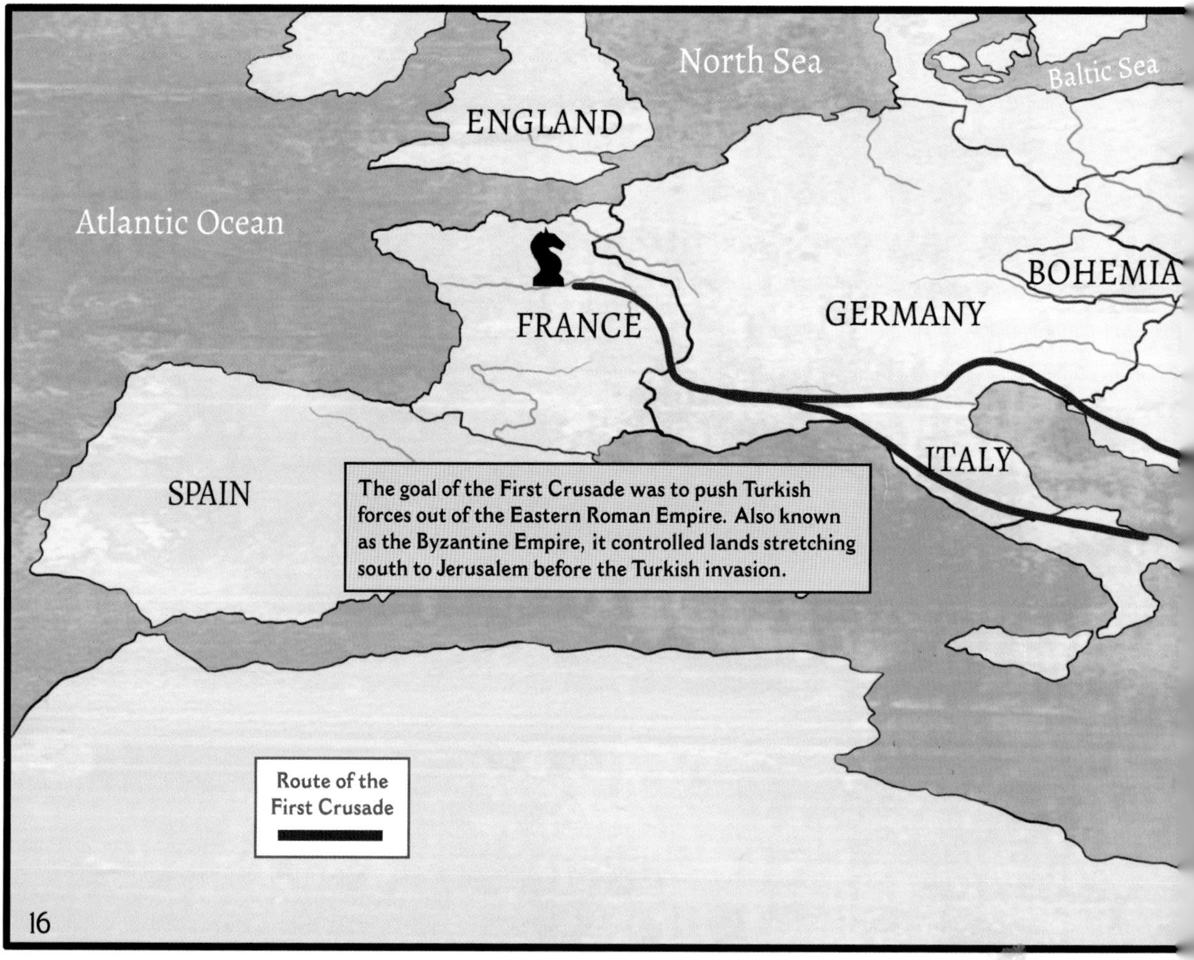
North Sea
Baltic Sea
ENGLAND
Atlantic Ocean
BOHEMIA
FRANCE
GERMANY
ITALY
SPAIN
The goal of the First Crusade was to push Turkish forces out of the Eastern Roman Empire. Also known as the Byzantine Empire, it controlled lands stretching south to Jerusalem before the Turkish invasion.
Route of the First Crusade

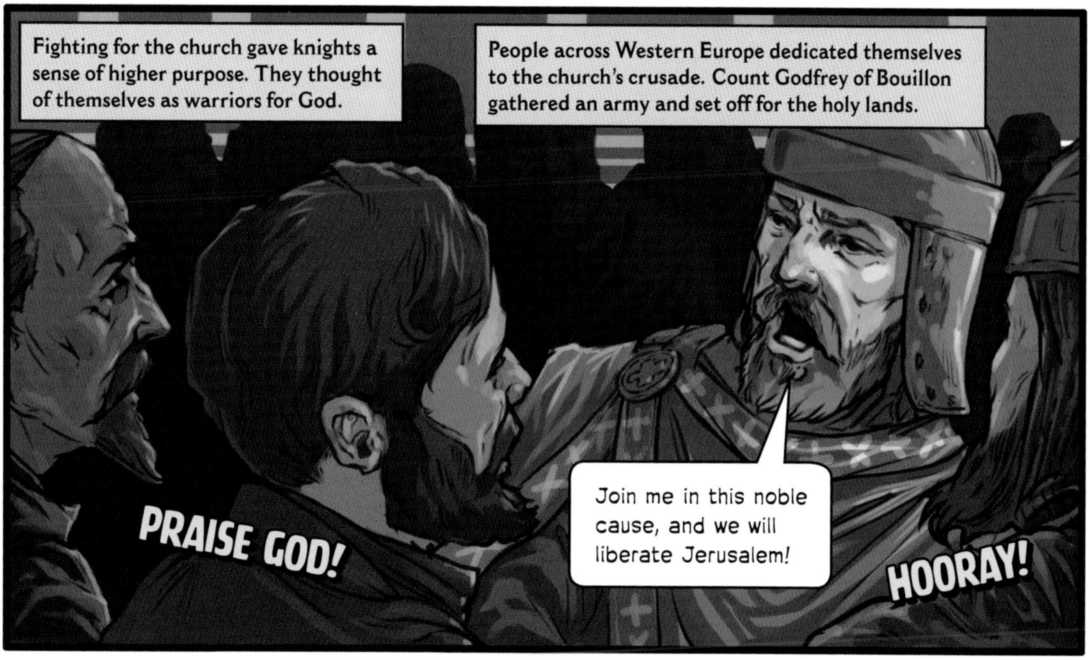
Fighting for the church gave knights a sense of higher purpose. They thought of themselves as warriors for God.
People across Western Europe dedicated themselves to the church's crusade. Count Godfrey of Bouillon gathered an army and set off for the holy lands.
PRAISE GOD!
Join me in this noble cause, and we will liberate Jerusalem!
HOORAY!

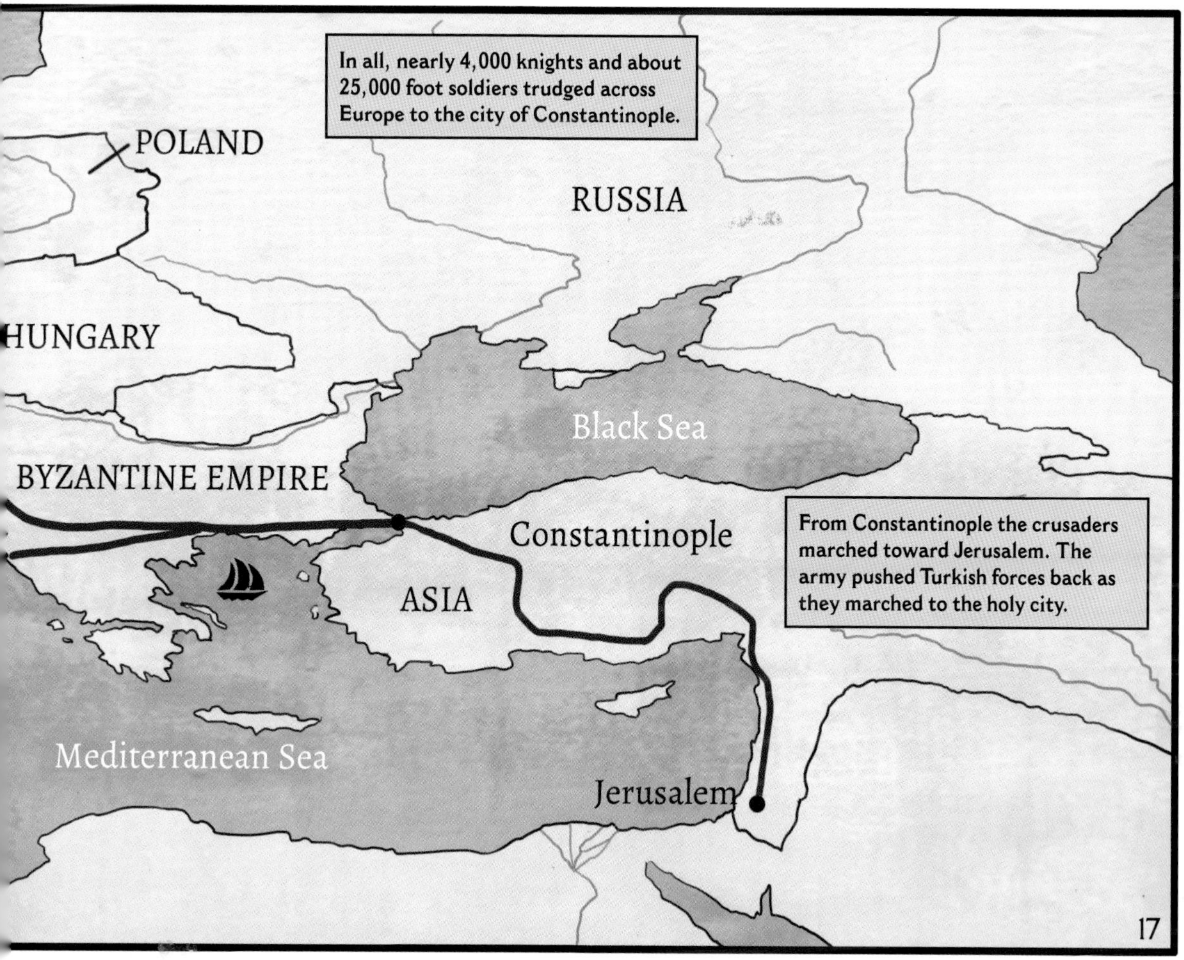
In all, nearly 4,000 knights and about 25,000 foot soldiers trudged across Europe to the city of Constantinople.
POLAND
RUSSIA
HUNGARY
Black Sea
BYZANTINE EMPIRE
Constantinople
ASIA
From Constantinople the crusaders marched toward Jerusalem. The army pushed Turkish forces back as they marched to the holy city.
Mediterranean Sea
Jerusalem

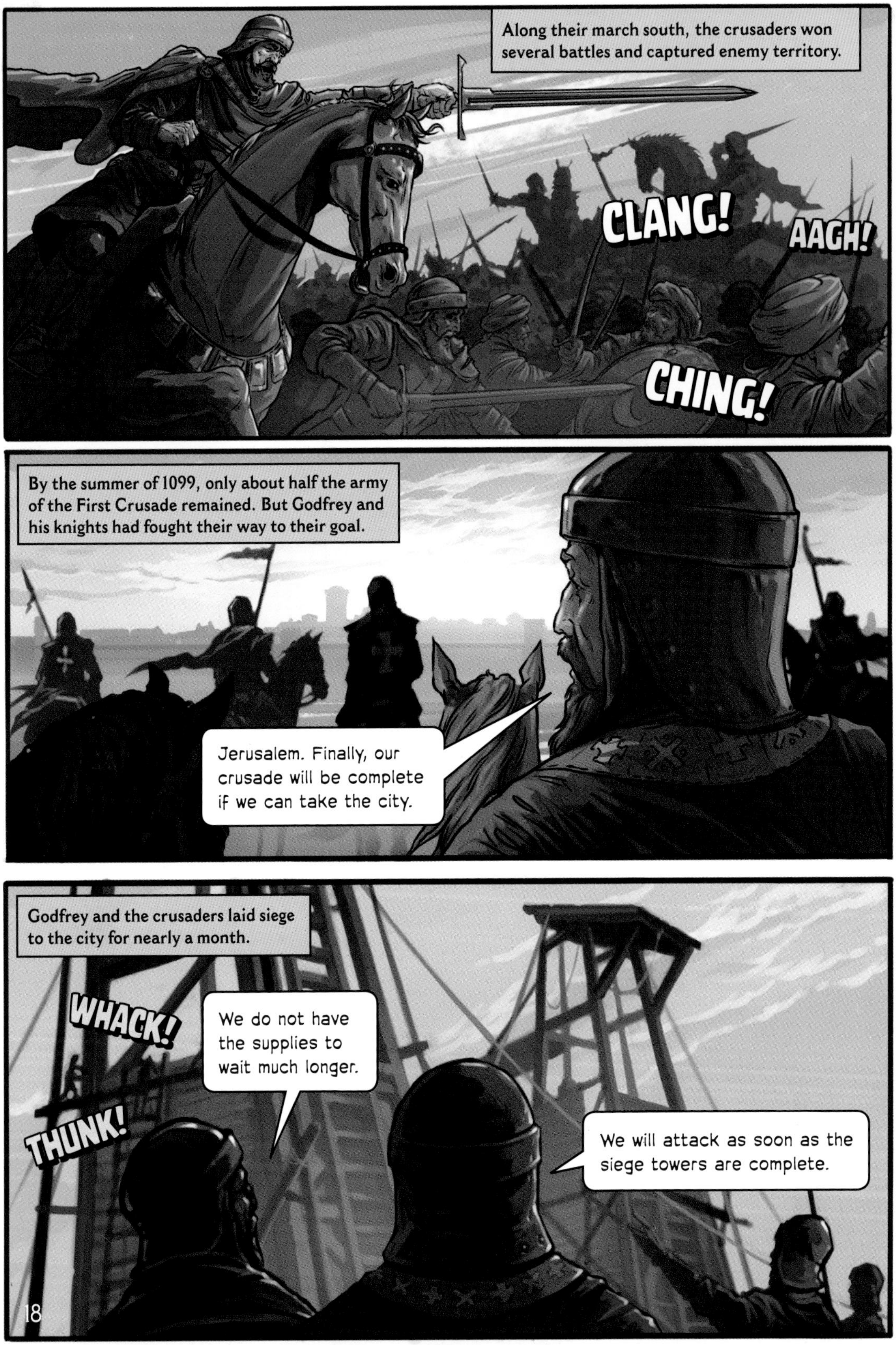
Along their march south, the crusaders won several battles and captured enemy territory.
CLANG!
AAGH!
CHING!
By the summer of 1099, only about half the army of the First Crusade remained. But Godfrey and his knights had fought their way to their goal.
Jerusalem. Finally, our crusade will be complete if we can take the city.
Godfrey and the crusaders laid siege to the city for nearly a month.
WHACK!
THUNK!
We do not have the supplies to wait much longer.
We will attack as soon as the siege towers are complete.

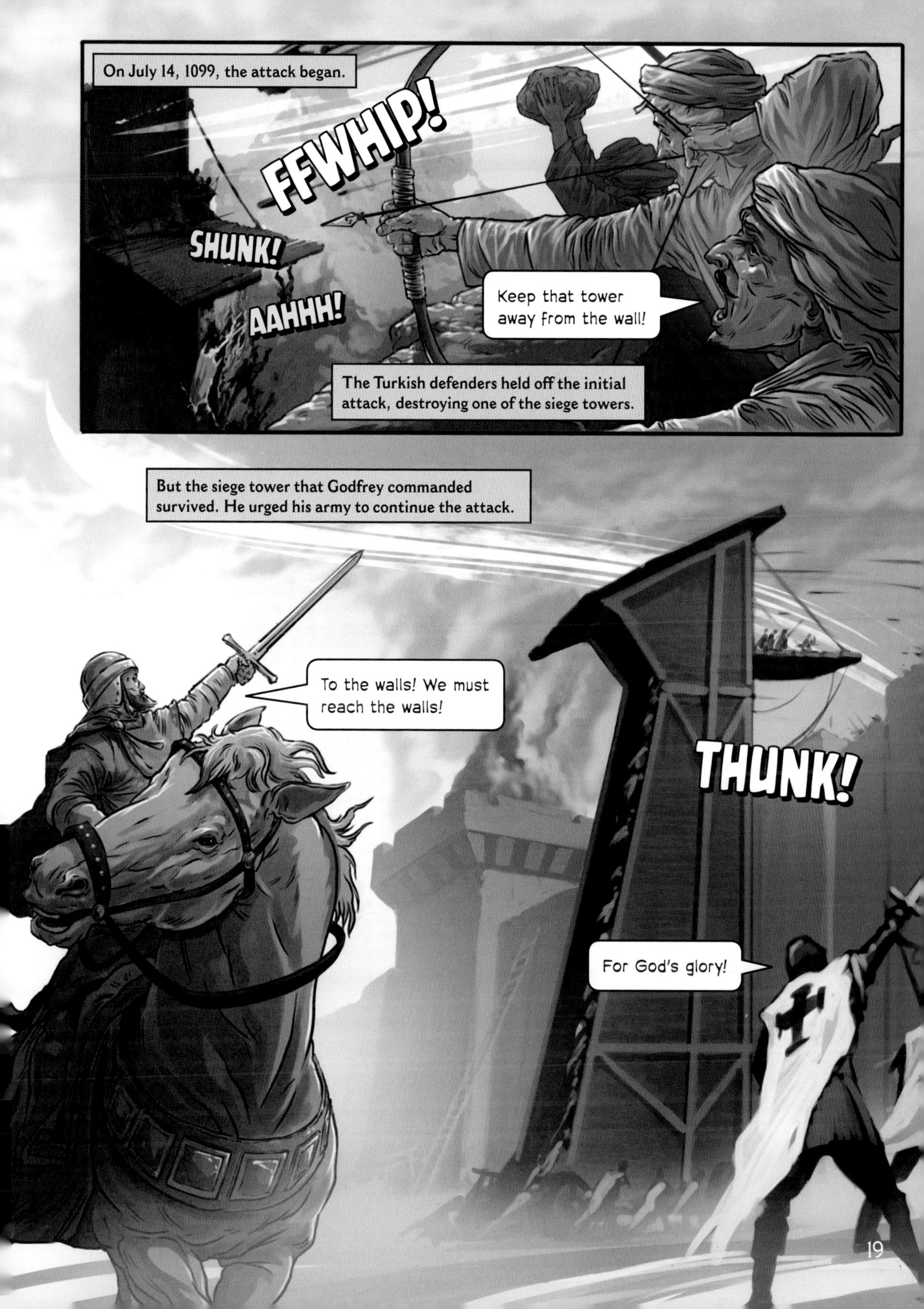
On July 14, 1099, the attack began.
FFWHIP!
SHUNK!
AAHHH!
Keep that tower away from the wall!
The Turkish defenders held off the initial attack, destroying one of the siege towers.
But the siege tower that Godfrey commanded survived. He urged his army to continue the attack.
To the walls! We must reach the walls!
THUNK!
For God's glory!

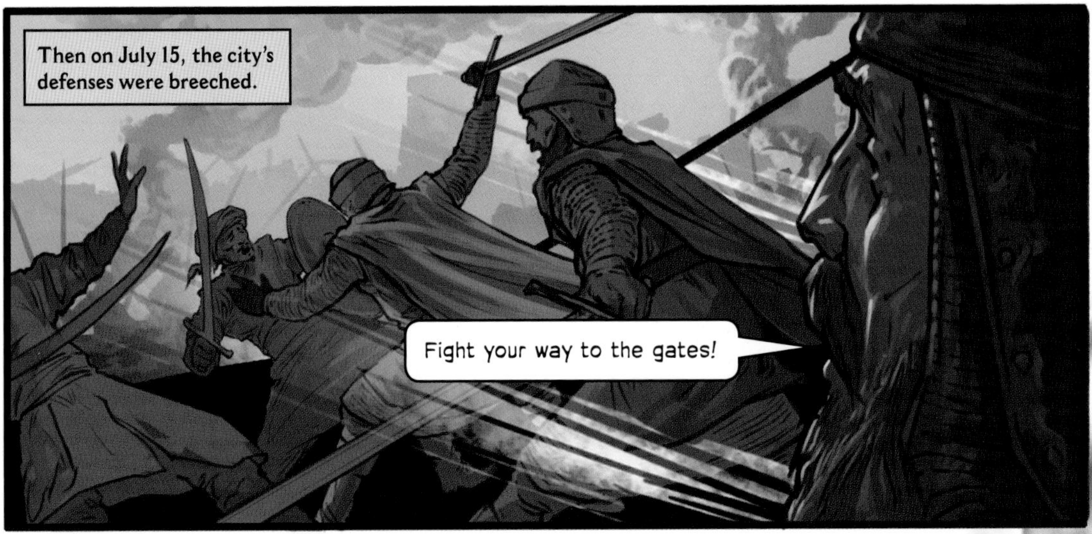
Then on July 15, the city's defenses were breeched.
Fight your way to the gates!

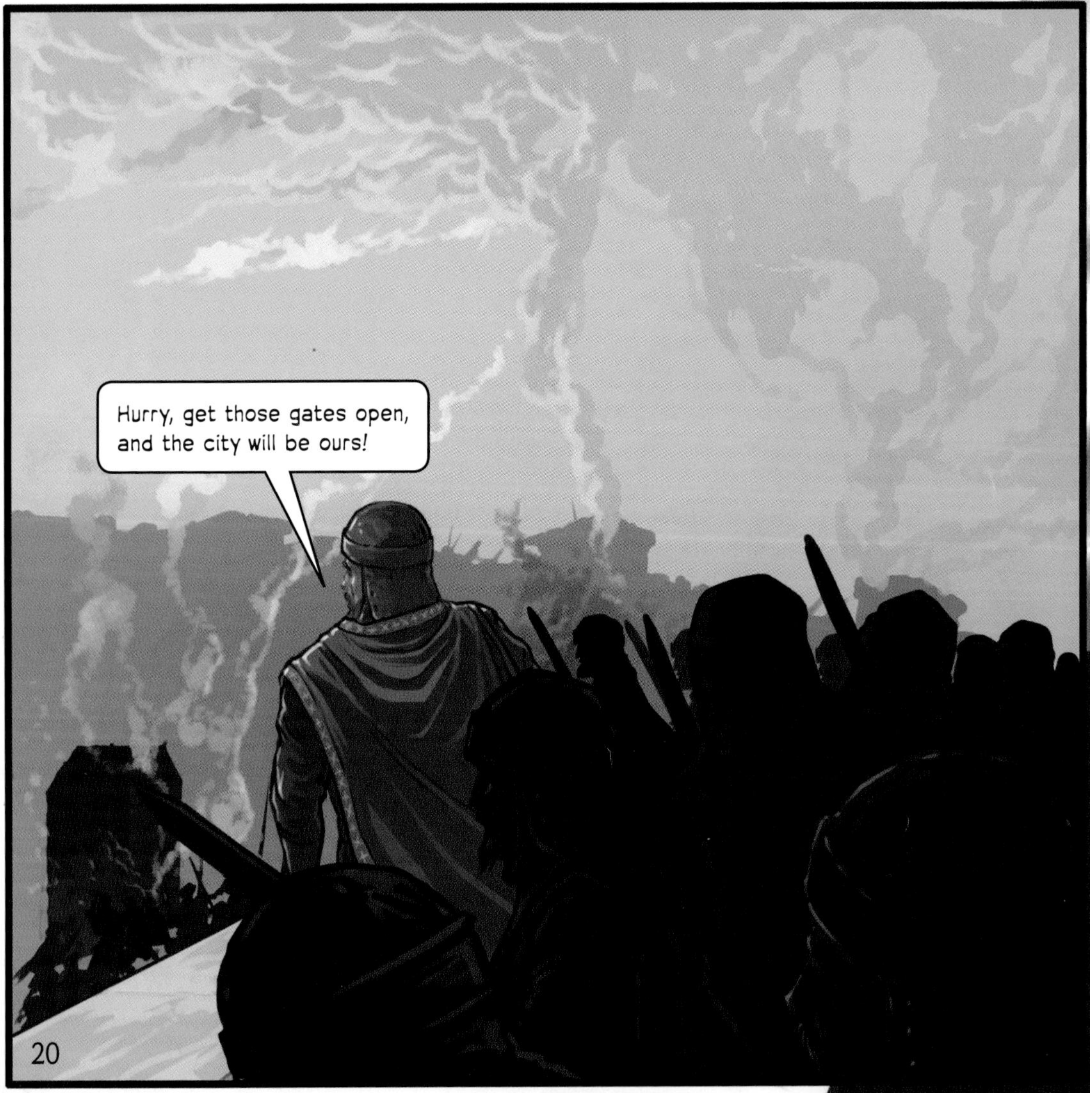
Hurry, get those gates open, and the city will be ours!

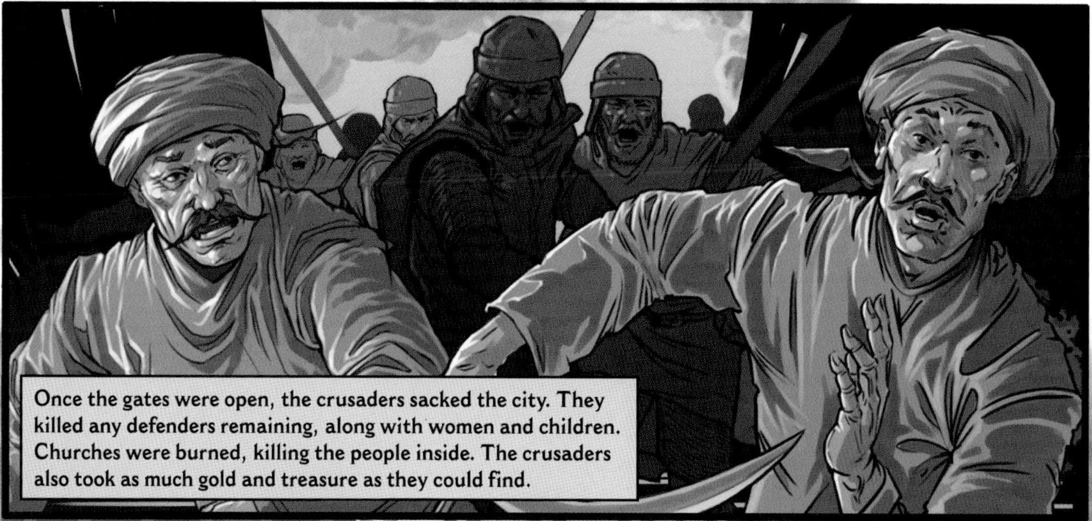
Once the gates were open, the crusaders sacked the city. They killed any defenders remaining, along with women and children. Churches were burned, killing the people inside. The crusaders also took as much gold and treasure as they could find.

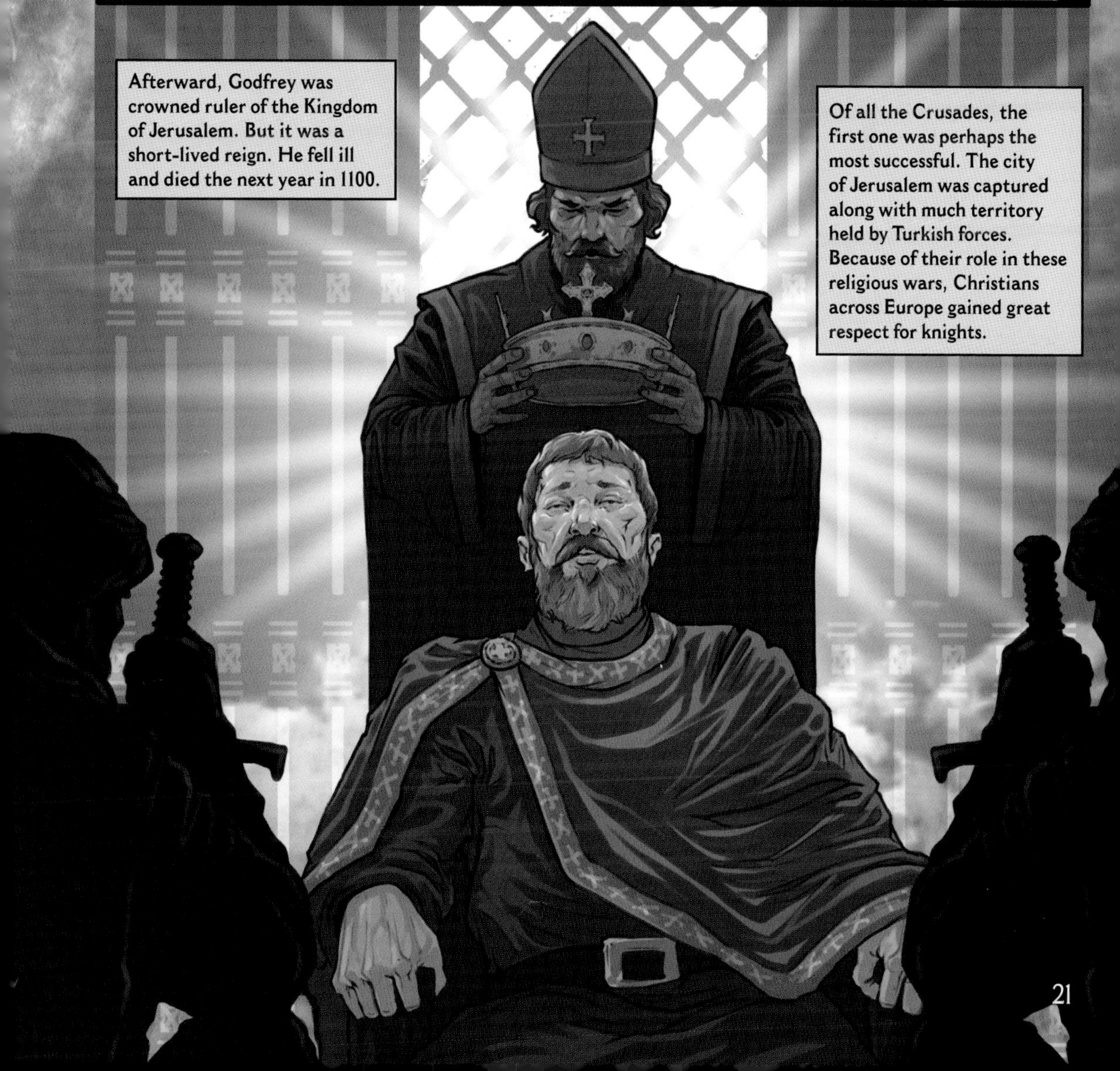
Afterward, Godfrey was crowned ruler of the Kingdom of Jerusalem. But it was a short-lived reign. He fell ill and died the next year in 1100.
Of all the Crusades, the first one was perhaps the most successful. The city of Jerusalem was captured along with much territory held by Turkish forces. Because of their role in these religious wars, Christians across Europe gained great respect for knights.

THE BATTLE OF CRÉCY

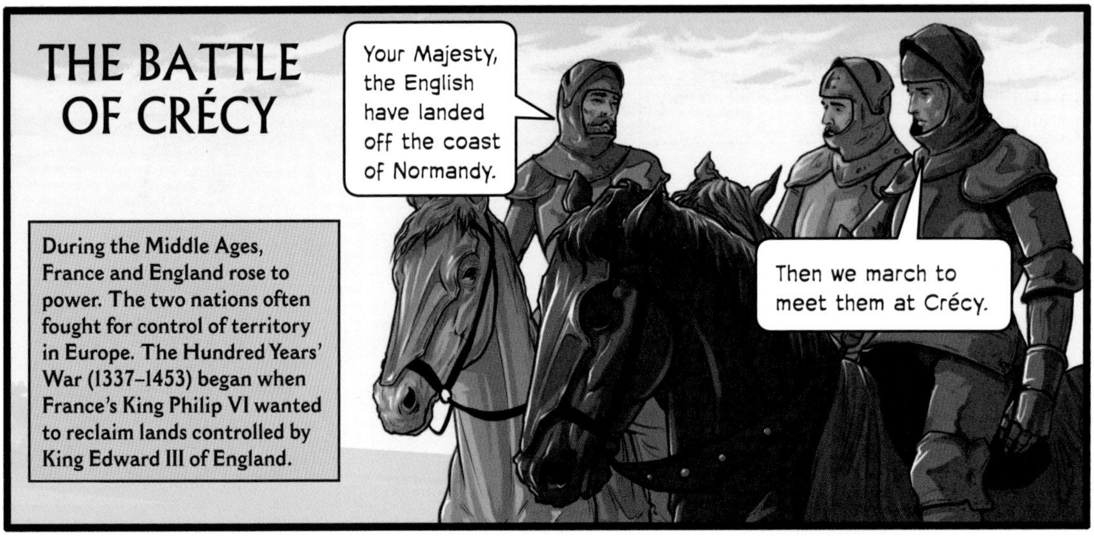
During the Middle Ages, France and England rose to power. The two nations often fought for control of territory in Europe. The Hundred Years' War (1337–1453) began when France's King Philip VI wanted to reclaim lands controlled by King Edward III of England.
Your Majesty, the English have landed off the coast of Normandy.
Then we march to meet them at Crécy.

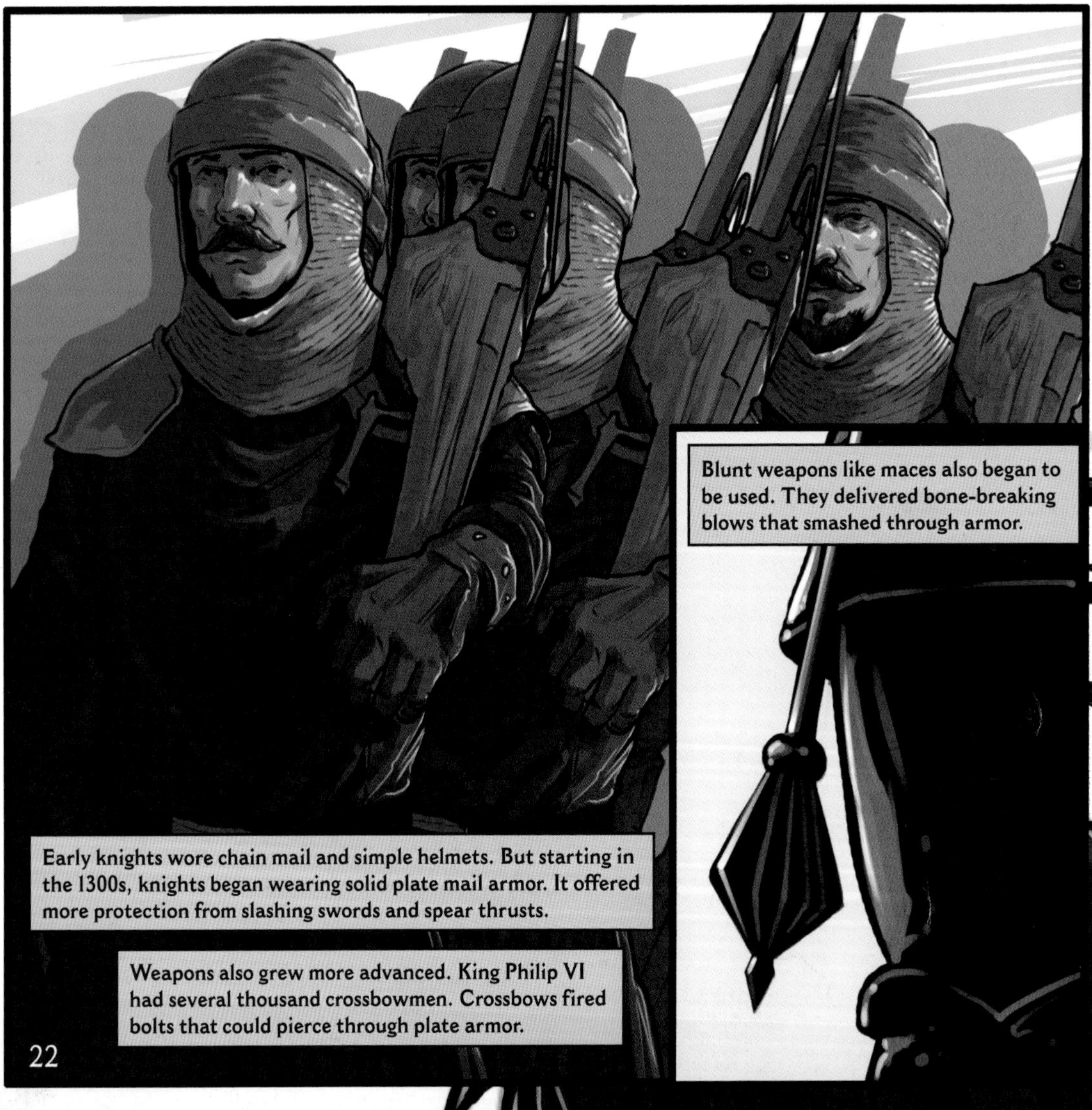
Early knights wore chain mail and simple helmets. But starting in the 1300s, knights began wearing solid plate mail armor. It offered more protection from slashing swords and spear thrusts.
Weapons also grew more advanced. King Philip VI had several thousand crossbowmen. Crossbows fired bolts that could pierce through plate armor.
Blunt weapons like maces also began to be used. They delivered bone-breaking blows that smashed through armor.

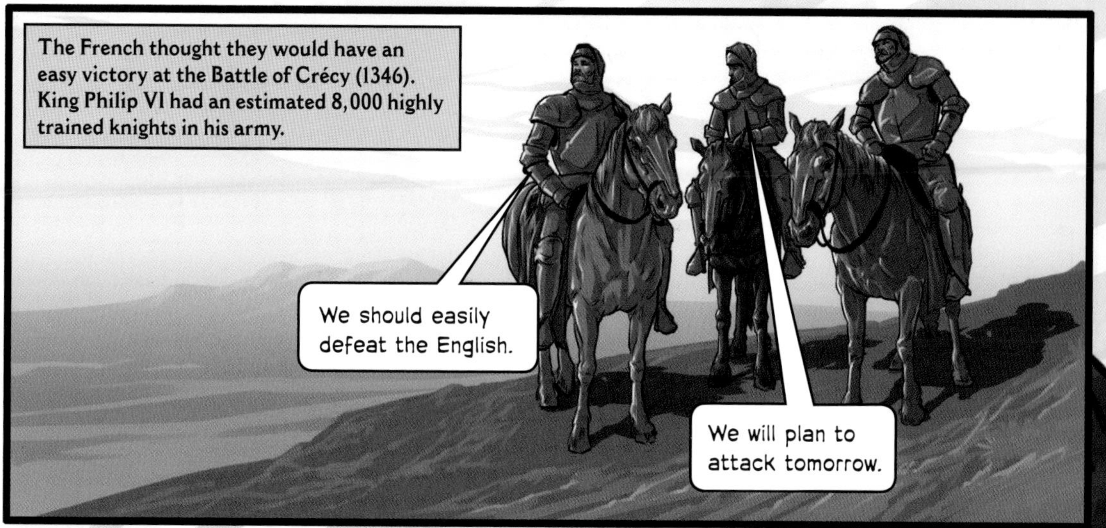
The French thought they would have an easy victory at the Battle of Crécy (1346). King Philip VI had an estimated 8,000 highly trained knights in his army.
We should easily defeat the English.
We will plan to attack tomorrow.

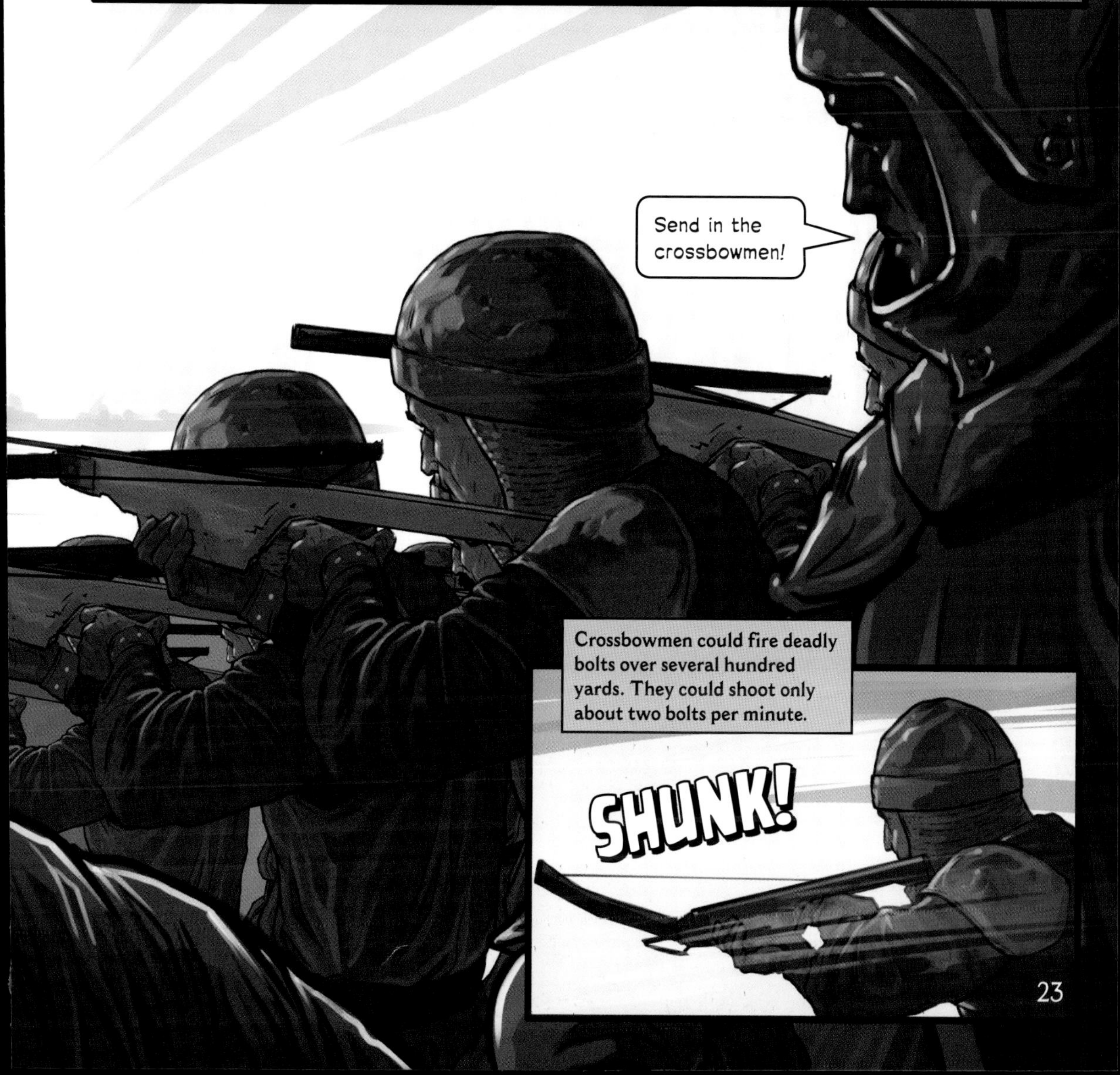
Send in the crossbowmen!
Crossbowmen could fire deadly bolts over several hundred yards. They could shoot only about two bolts per minute.
SHUNK!

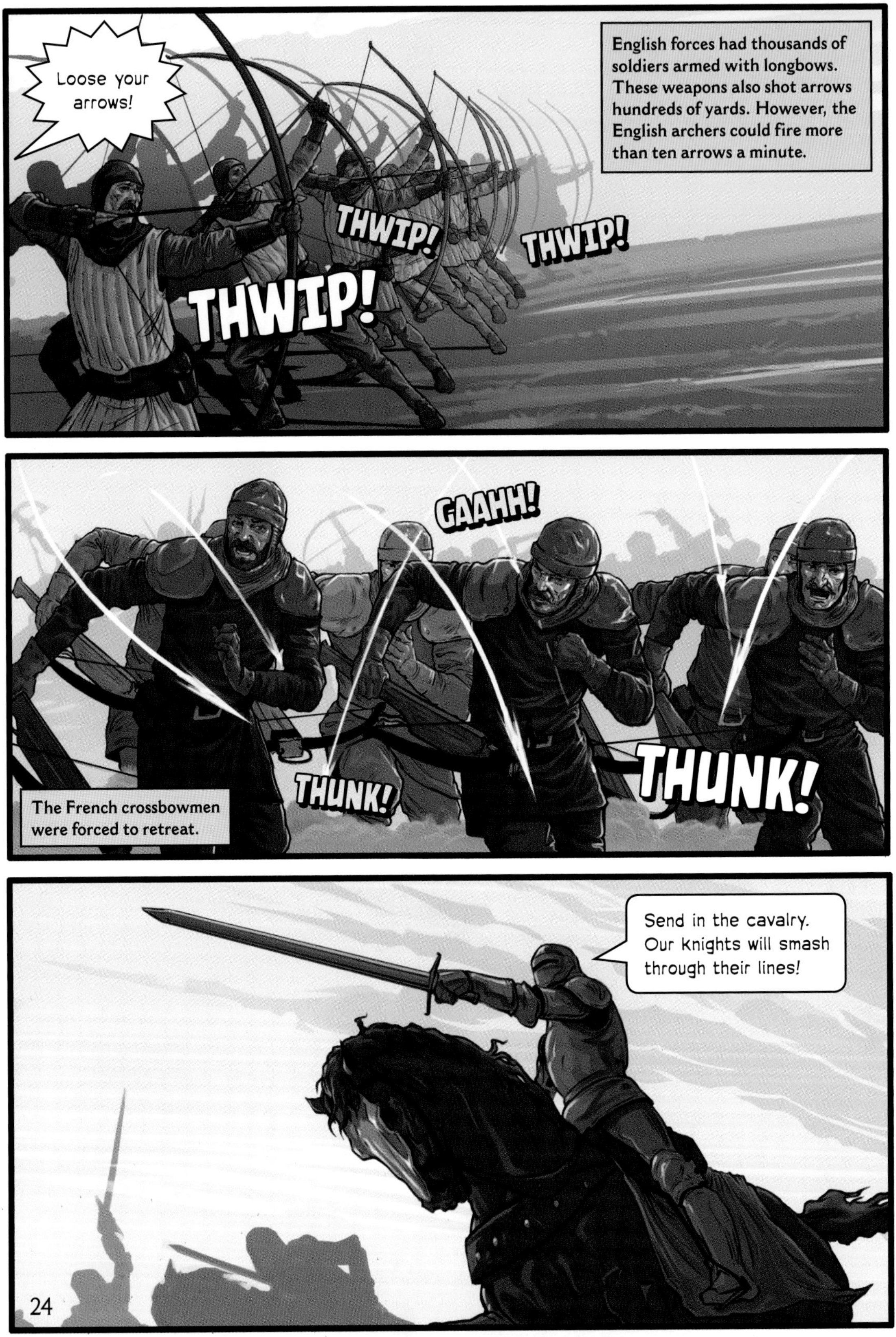
Loose your arrows!
English forces had thousands of soldiers armed with longbows. These weapons also shot arrows hundreds of yards. However, the English archers could fire more than ten arrows a minute.
THWIP!
THWIP!
THWIP!
GAAHH!
The French crossbowmen were forced to retreat.
THUNK!
THUNK!
Send in the cavalry. Our knights will smash through their lines!

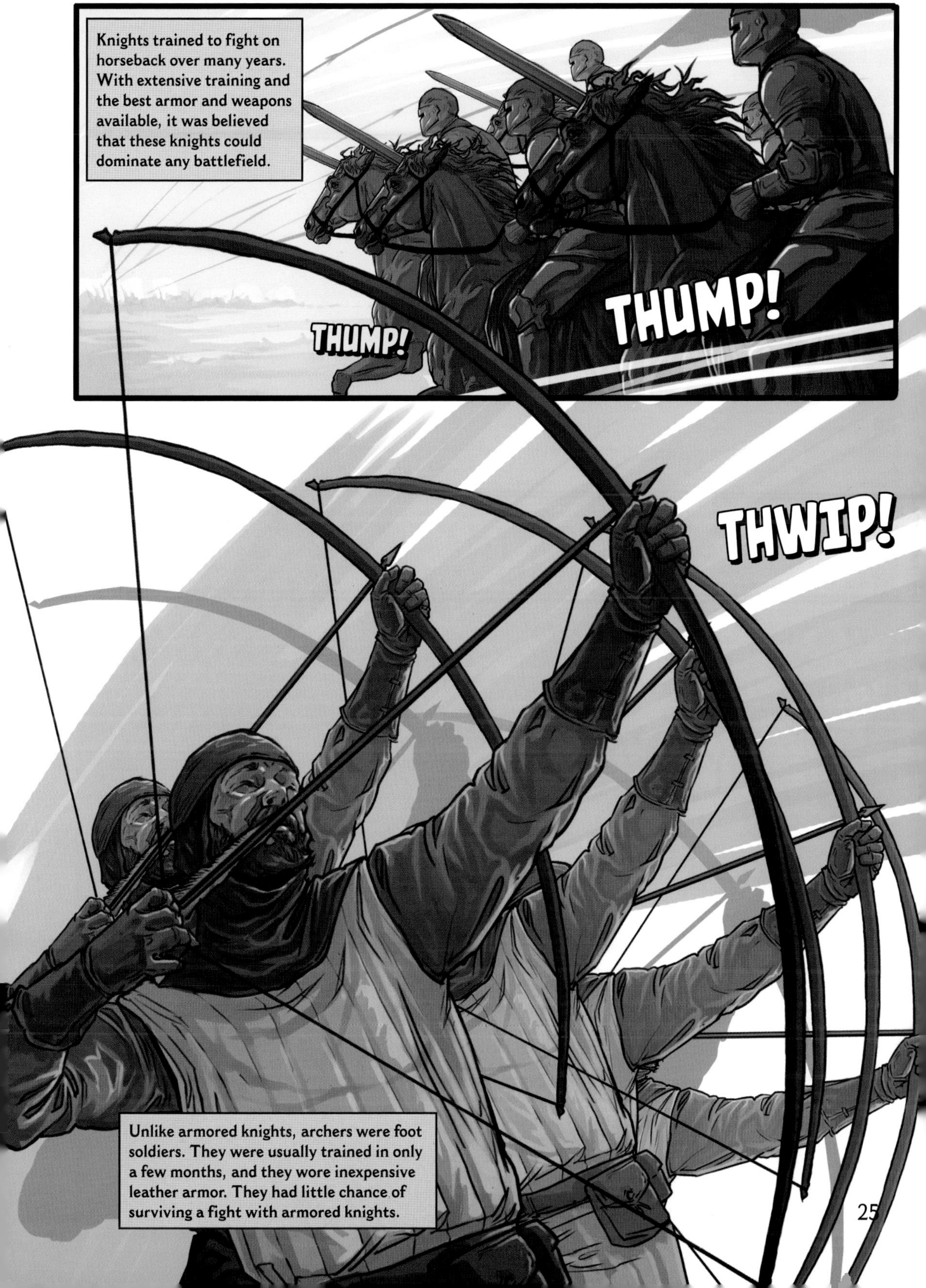
Knights trained to fight on horseback over many years. With extensive training and the best armor and weapons available, it was believed that these knights could dominate any battlefield.
THUMP!
THUMP!
THWIP!
Unlike armored knights, archers were foot soldiers. They were usually trained in only a few months, and they wore inexpensive leather armor. They had little chance of surviving a fight with armored knights.

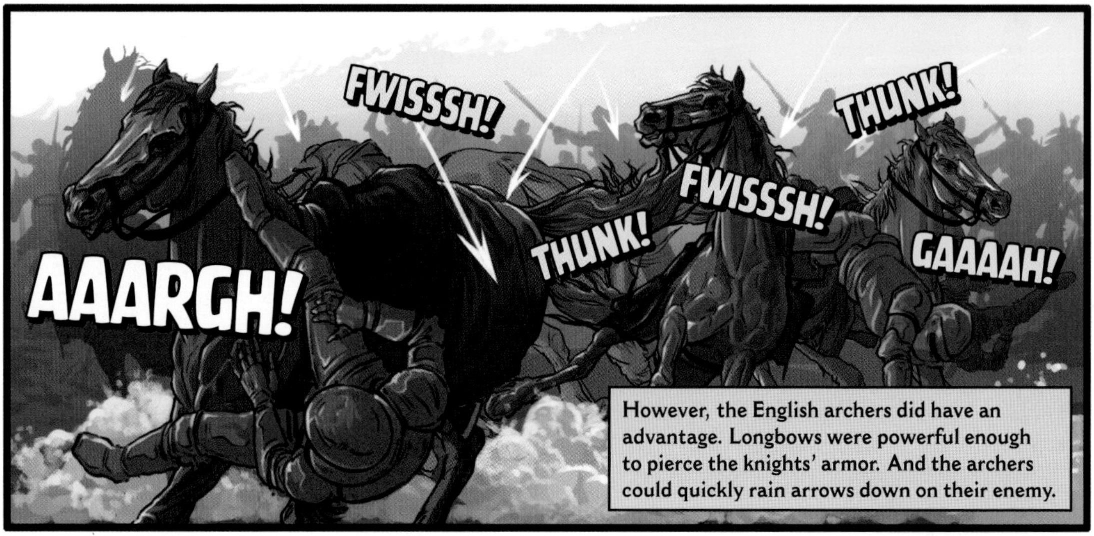
FWISSSH!
THUNK!
FWISSSH!
THUNK!
AAARGH!
GAAAAH!
However, the English archers did have an advantage. Longbows were powerful enough to pierce the knights' armor. And the archers could quickly rain arrows down on their enemy.

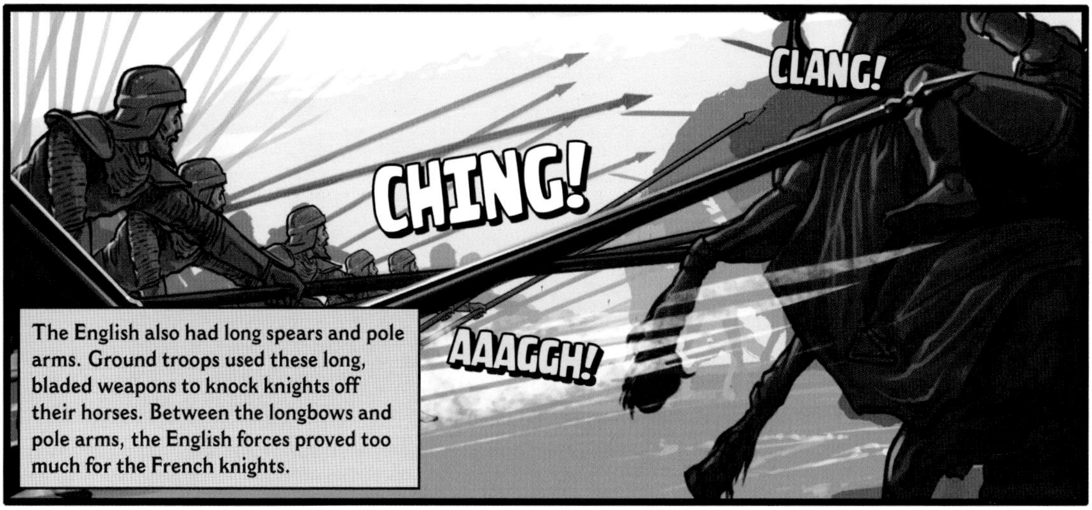
CLANG!
CHING!
The English also had long spears and pole arms. Ground troops used these long, bladed weapons to knock knights off their horses. Between the longbows and pole arms, the English forces proved too much for the French knights.
AAAGGH!

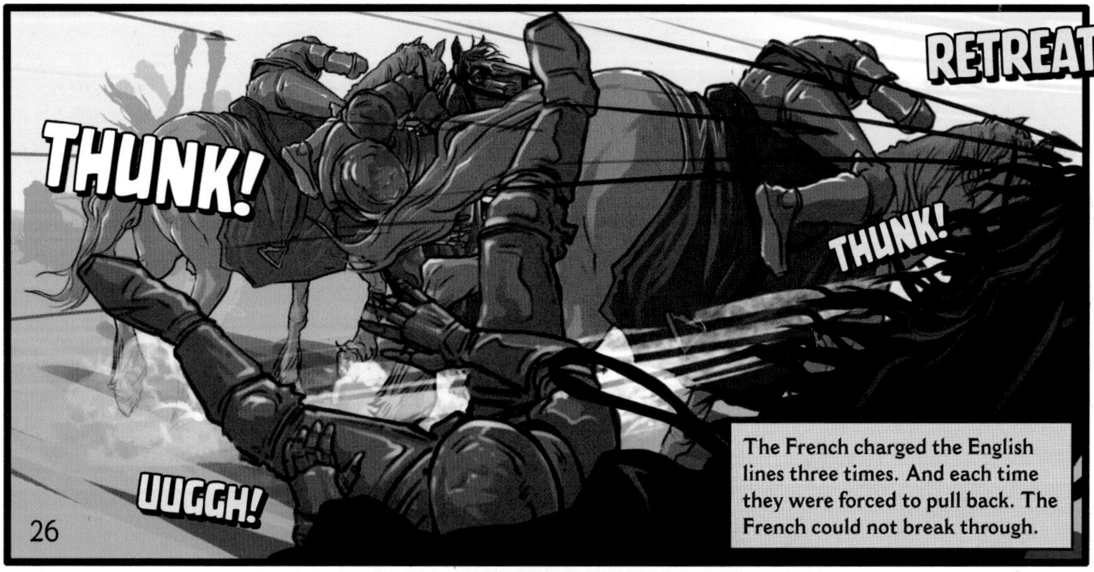
RETREAT!
THUNK!
THUNK!
UUGGH!
The French charged the English lines three times. And each time they were forced to pull back. The French could not break through.

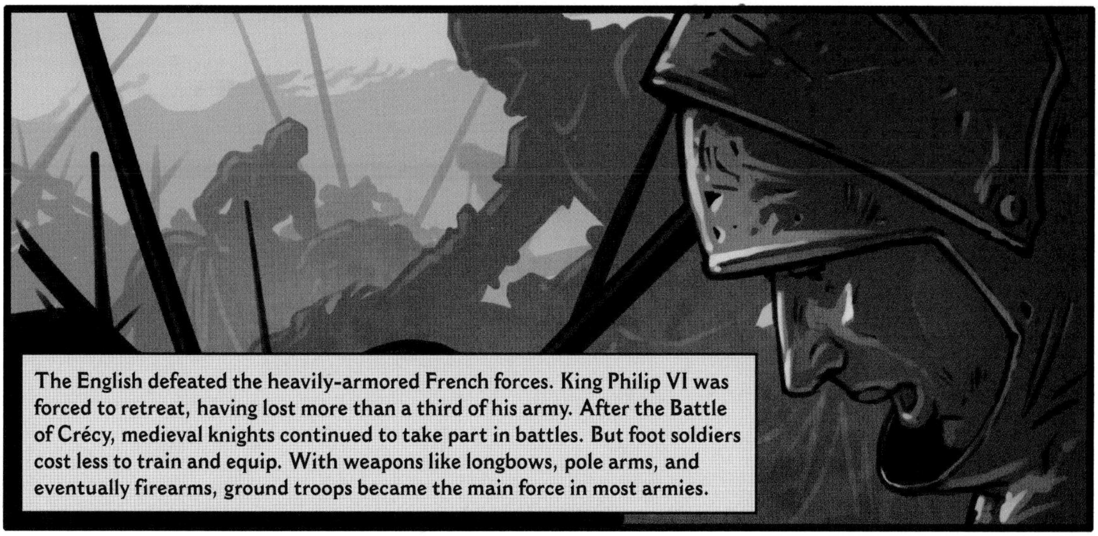
The English defeated the heavily-armored French forces. King Philip VI was forced to retreat, having lost more than a third of his army. After the Battle of Crécy, medieval knights continued to take part in battles. But foot soldiers cost less to train and equip. With weapons like longbows, pole arms, and eventually firearms, ground troops became the main force in most armies.

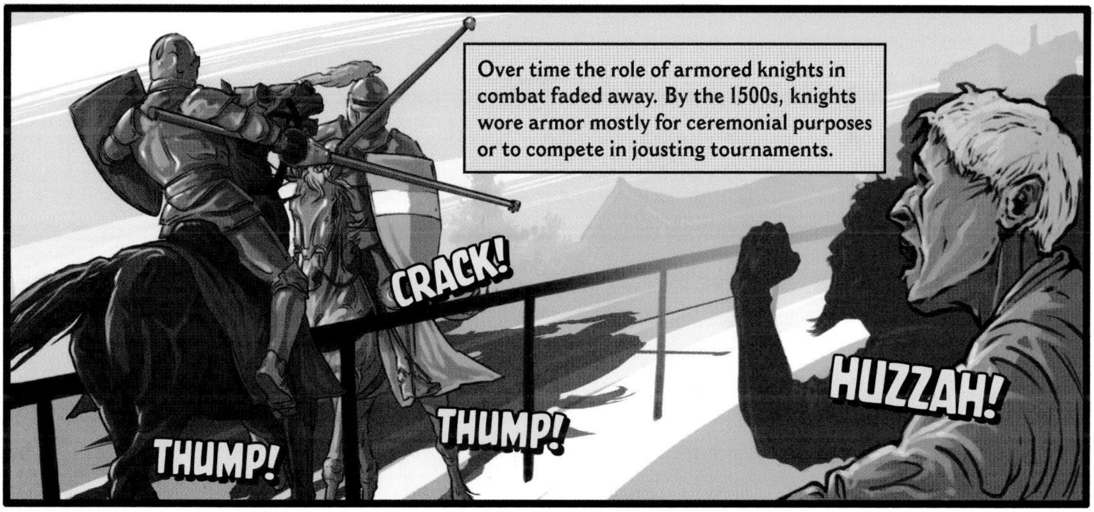
Over time the role of armored knights in combat faded away. By the 1500s, knights wore armor mostly for ceremonial purposes or to compete in jousting tournaments.
CRACK!
HUZZAH!
THUMP!
THUMP!

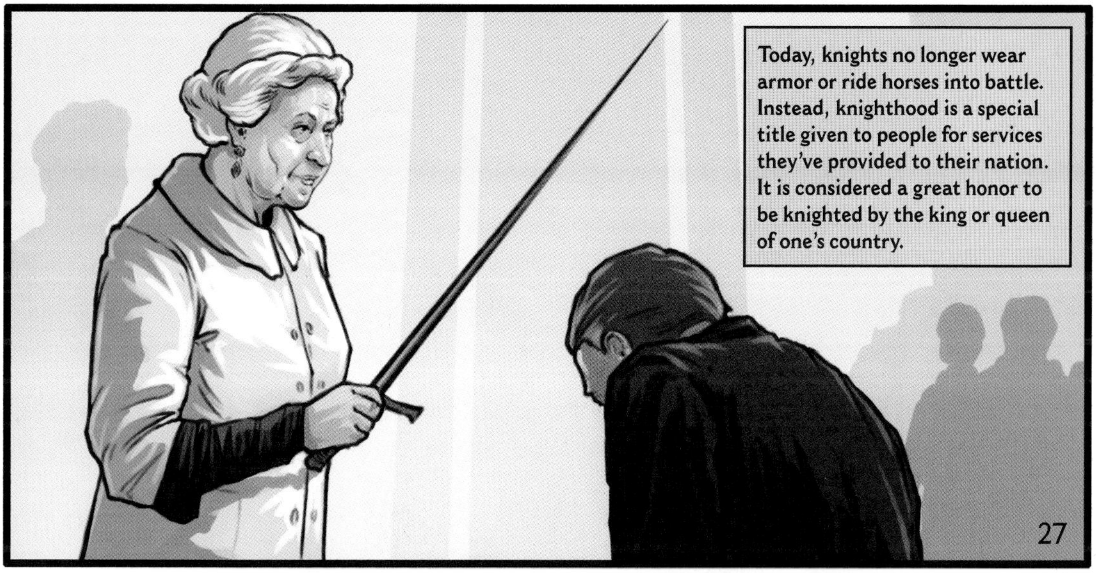
Today, knights no longer wear armor or ride horses into battle. Instead, knighthood is a special title given to people for services they've provided to their nation. It is considered a great honor to be knighted by the king or queen of one's country.

MORE ABOUT
MEDIEVAL KNIGHTS

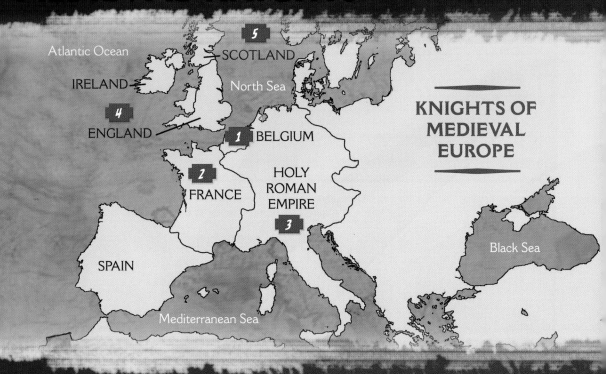

Atlantic Ocean

SCOTLAND

IRELAND

North Sea

ENGLAND

BELGIUM

FRANCE

HOLY
ROMAN
EMPIRE

SPAIN

Black Sea

Mediterranean Sea

**KNIGHTS OF
MEDIEVAL
EUROPE**

1 Belgium

Godfrey of Bouillon (1060–1100)
Belgian Knight who took part in the First
Crusade (1095–1099). He helped lead the
crusaders in the capture of Jerusalem,
and for a brief time he became its ruler.

2 France

Knights Templar (1119—1312)
Religious order founded by French knight Hugues
de Payens. This group of knights was strongly
connected to the Crusades. They made vows of
poverty and were not allowed to drink or swear.
After the last crusade failed, support for them faded.

3 Holy Roman Empire

Teutonic Knights (1190–?)
Religious order founded to help pilgrims traveling to the
Holy Land. Originally they established hospitals to help
the injured, but grew into a military force over time.
The majority of its members were from Germany.

4 England

Sir William Marshal (1147–1219)
Also known as the first Earl of Pembroke.
English knight who first earned fame on the
tournament field. He also served five English
kings, including King Richard the Lionhearted.

5 Scotland

Sir James Douglas (1289–1330)
Also known as Sir James the Good by
the Scots and James the Black by the English.
Scottish knight who fought during the first
War of Scottish Independence.

ARMOR ADVANCEMENTS

Medieval knights always wore armor for protection in battle. But over time, their armor changed to better protect them from more advanced weaponry.

1100s AD

The main protection for early knights was chain mail armor, made of small interlocking rings of iron. A long chain mail shirt called a hauberk hung down to cover a knight's upper thighs. Hauberks often had a metal coif, or hood, as well. Knights usually wore a cone-shaped helmet and carried a large shield.

1200s AD

In the 1200s knights began adding metal plates to help protect certain areas like the shoulders and chest. Grieves, or shin armor, helped protect the legs. Knights also wore full helmets and used smaller shields that were easier to carry while riding on horseback.

1400s AD

By the mid-1400s knights were wearing suits of full plate armor. These metal suits completely covered a knight's body for full protection. Helmets had a visor that could be lifted up to see better. Plated gloves called gauntlets were worn to protect the hands. A metal wrapper called a gorget was worn around the neck to protect a knight's throat from lance blows.

GLOSSARY

bolt (BOHLT)—a short, heavy arrow used for a crossbow

cavalry (KA-vuhl-ree)—soldiers who travel and fight on horseback

feudal system (FYOOD-uhl SIS-tuhm)—a system of government in the Middle Ages in which knights received land for their military service; common people worked the land for the knight

fief (FEEF)—a piece of land owned and controlled by a lord

infantry (IN-fuhn-tree)—soldiers who travel and fight on foot

lance (LANSS)—a long, spear-like weapon

melee (MEY-ley)—a chaotic hand-to-hand battle with many opponents

Middle Ages (MID-uhl AYJ-uhss)—a period of time in Europe from about AD 500 to 1500

page (PAYJ)—a young man in service to a member of a royal court or to a knight

siege (SEEJ)—an attack designed to surround a fort or city to cut it off from supplies or help

tournament (TUR-nuh-muhnt)—a series of matches or contests between several players or teams, ending in one winner

READ MORE

Ganeri, Anita. *How to Live Like a Medieval Knight.* How to Live Like... . Minneapolis: Hungry Tomato, 2016.

Lassieur, Allison. *Medieval Knight Science: Armor, Weapons, and Siege Warfare.* Warrior Science. North Mankato, Minn.: Capstone Press, 2017.

O'Brien, Cynthia. *Your Guide to Knights and the Age of Chivalry.* Destination: Middle Ages. New York: Crabtree Publishing, 2017.

CRITICAL THINKING QUESTIONS

- Knights were expected to be chivalrous, meaning they had to be honorable and defend those in need. Which warrior mentioned in the book do you feel was the most chivalrous knight? Explain your answer.

- Think about the stories of knights in this book. How do they compare to what you knew about knights before? In what ways has your view of medieval knights changed after reading this book?

- Knights often went on quests or performed heroic deeds to earn fame. If you were a knight in the modern world, what would you do to become famous? Remember that knights were expected to live by a code of chivalry.

INTERNET SITES

Use Facthound to find Internet sites related to this book.

Visit *www.facthound.com*

Just type in 9781543555011 and go.

INDEX